CW01310145

Successful Parenting –

The Four Step

Approach

by

Dr. Geoff Thorley

authorHOUSE™

1663 LIBERTY DRIVE, SUITE 200
BLOOMINGTON, INDIANA 47403
(800) 839-8640
WWW.AUTHORHOUSE.COM

© 2005 Dr. Geoff Thorley. All Rights Reserved.

No part of this book may be reproduced, stored in a retrieval system, or transmitted by any means without the written permission of the author.

First published by AuthorHouse 12/06/05

ISBN: 1-4259-0762-8 (e)
ISBN: 1-4208-8149-3 (sc)

Printed in the United States of America
Bloomington, Indiana

This book is printed on acid-free paper.

Dedication

To Mark, Michael, Caroline and Oliver

CONTENTS

INTRODUCTION ix
STEP 1 PARENTAL ATTITUDES AND EXPECTATIONS...1
   Nature and nurture 2
   Parental expectations 17
STEP 2 PARENTING STYLE 23
   Ways of understanding people and the world 24
   Attachment 29
   Positive and negative talk 32
   Independence 34
   Parenting style 35
   Key moments 43
   Conflicts of parenting style 45
   Marital issues 47
STEP 3 THE WORLD OF YOUNG PEOPLE 51
   The Family 51
   Marital relationships 63
   School 66
   Neighbourhoods 77
   Child and youth culture 82
   Spiritual, moral and religious matters 85
   Biological and physical aspects 87
STEP 4 TECHNIQUES AND STRATEGIES 95
   The self v others 96
   What is behaviour? 98
   Describing target behaviour and emotions 99
   Analysing behaviour – knowing your ABC 100

Prioritising problems 114
Recording and measuring 116
Specific techniques.. 117
    Reinforcement 118
    Token systems 124
    Allowances... 137
  Punishment 138
    Withdrawing privileges 139
    Punishing events 141
    Verbal reprimands....................................... 142
    Time out 143
    Physical punishment................................... 147
REFERENCES 151

INTRODUCTION

Parenting can be tough but never boring. I have always seen it as similar to a long, adventurous journey, during which peoples' reactions to events and situations along the way make for either a pleasurable or miserable time for all involved. An adventurous journey differs from a one-week package holiday in a number of ways. With the package holiday, you have limited time and expect things to run to plan. The long adventurous holiday is different. It needs careful planning and re-planning. You might have an ultimate destination but are prepared to change this if circumstances warrant it. You would want to take time to enjoy occasional diversions if they look interesting. You would expect problems and perhaps disasters along the way. You may still be surprised and devastated if they occur but be better able to take them in your stride than if you blinded yourself to the possibility of such things ever happening. You might try to enjoy any pleasant, unexpected event and even search out the interesting and unusual. Finally, looking back, it might be the case that the journey itself was just as interesting and satisfying as any final destination.

I hope that **THE FOUR-STEP APPROACH** will serve as a welcome travel guide and companion for you. The ideas for the book stem from my work as a clinical child psychologist over the past 20 years. Over this period, I became aware that effective parenting isn't just about learning particular parenting techniques such as star charts, Time Out etc. and in any case, parents had become increasingly knowledgeable and knew many of the techniques anyway. What became clear to me is that many parents lack an appropriate parenting philosophy or framework. More often than not, if they did have a framework, it wasn't helping, wasn't satisfying and was resulting in too many battles with their children. I have developed **The FOUR-STEP APPROACH** from my clinical practice but have adapted it to meet the needs of everyday parenting.

I have been particularly spurred on to write this book because I see parenting as a difficult job, and getting more difficult. Despite this, I am saddened that parents are too readily blamed for problems presented by young people. An article I read by the UK Chief Inspector of Schools is typical of this tendency: he claimed that 5-year-olds were now more disruptive at school and that this was because of the failure of parents to impose discipline at home (Sunday Telegraph, 31st August 2003). It seems unreasonable to me to lay all of the blame onto parents. He may have overlooked the fact that there is a growing trend for children to start school earlier. Parents have less time with their children before they enter schools that are also becoming more demanding on young people. In 1970/71, only 20% of the under-5s in the UK attended school whereas in 2000/2001 the figure was 60% (Social Trends, 2002). Added to this, more and more parents are working. Forty six per cent of mothers with children now work full or part-time. This rises to 65% for mothers with children of 10 years and under (Social Trends, 1995). The UK has the highest proportion of mothers in work compared to the rest of the EU. I do not necessarily see these trends as bad, but I do see them as a product of the way our society is developing. I realise that we need a more educated workforce and we need more and more people to work in jobs created by our expanding economy. In my view, if parents are not always coming up with the goods it is a problem that we are all responsible for and instead of blaming parents, it would be better to do more to support them.

I am often asked if I believe parenting is more difficult now than in the past. My view is that parenting has always been difficult but the types of difficulty have changed over time. Just 70 years ago, the priority for many parents in the UK (as it still is in many developing countries), was to keep their children fed and healthy. Now the tasks are different but, arguably, just as demanding. This is partly due, I think, to the pace of social and economic change. At time of great change, parenting tasks change very quickly to the extent that there is frequently a skills gap for many parents. In other words, it is difficult for parents to adjust and develop their skills to meet the needs of a rapidly changing world. The changes can happen so quickly that people are not adequately prepared for them. Until recently, most people, when they were children, might have imagined growing up, marrying the same person for life and having children within that marriage. They would have learned about parenting from their own experiences with their parents, through observing how their friends are parented and more generally, learning about being a parent through watching films and TV. In recent decades, many parents have had to abandon these expectations and learn, for example, how to parent as single people, be effective step-parents and foster parents or parent adopted children. In addition to these new parenting challenges, the world of work and education for both parents and children have undergone significant changes which also affect parenting. Education is a good example where significant changes have taken place, particularly the extended time young people remain in education and the implications this has for parenting. It is not only that children are enrolled at school at an earlier age, but also that they remain in education for longer. In 1982, just 13.6% of 18-year-olds in the UK were in higher education (University). The figure is now approximately 43%. Thus young people need parenting for much longer before becoming economically independent. Add to this the pressures on marriage, and it means that a growing number of young people are bought up in single parent households or reconstituted ones. As recently as 1981, just 13% of children were raised in single-parent households whereas in 2002 the figure was 26% (Social Trends, 2000). I won't analyse here all the reasons for this trend in the breakdown of marriage, but consider that in 1901, the life expectancy of women was 49 years, and for men it was 46 years (Social Trends, 1995). Now, the comparable figures are 80 years and 74 years. This means that in 1901, the average marriage lasted no longer than 30 years before the death of a spouse. Now, the average marriage could last twice as long, making it a much tougher business for couples to stay together.

In summary, there are considerable social changes which are having an impact on parents and their ability to bring up young people. The process of parenting has never been a smooth one and probably never will be. It is foolish to blame parents for all of the difficulties and, still worse, to accuse them of moral ineptitude. Raising children goes beyond the responsibilities of parents alone – everyone has a part to play in the process. This is why I think parents need help rather than a lack of support and understanding rather than condemnation. I hope that this book will play its part in helping parents do a job, which if done well, benefits us all.

THE FOUR-STEP APPROACH – A SUMMARY

My chief message is that you don't have to be a psychologist to become an effective parent. Also, there is no single recipe for everyone. Every child is a unique individual, as are each of its parents. It will be perfectly reasonable for some parents to aim to bring up their children to be psychologically and physically healthy, to enable them to become fully independent adults. For other parents with, for example, a learning disabled child or one with a significant mental health problem at the outset, there will be different objectives. The learning-disabled child may never be able to achieve full independence but it will be important to help him or her to learn how to make use of the support of others at key times.

The essence of the **Four-Step Approach** is the belief that in order for well-proven parenting techniques and strategies to work, parents need to ensure that they have the basic building blocks (Steps 1, 2 and 3) in place before applying specific techniques to shape and change behaviour of young people (Step 4). These building blocks are essentially to do with parents cultivating appropriate expectations of parenting (Step 1), developing a sound parenting style (Step 2), and becoming further informed by knowledge of social, biological, and psychological influences on their child (Step 3).

Steps 1, 2, and 3 make up a significant part of this book. This is in direct contrast to many books on parenting, which wholly focus on techniques such as rewards and punishments to achieve changes in behaviour, or promote certain aspects of development, such as self-esteem. Techniques are important, but in my view, are of limited value without an overall sense of parenting direction. This direction will be unique to each child, their parents, or carers.

> *Understanding the basic influences on how children develop into well-functioning adults is the key ingredient to effective parenting. If this is allowed inform and shape parenting practice, then I am of the firm view that any techniques or strategies will work more quickly and, better still, there will be less need for them in the first place.*

STEPS AND THEMES

Before introducing the Four Steps, it will be helpful to keep in mind what I call **Key Themes** that run throughout this book. The *steps* are vital ingredients of the **FOUR-STEP APPROACH,** and to my mind, have been, and always will be the cornerstone of parenting. The *themes* are transient, and are likely to change with time. This is because issues change with time. What is an issue in this decade may be less so in the next.. Right now, for example, there is controversy about the role of genetic influences on human behaviour. Time will probably help us all to arrive at some consensus belief as scientific knowledge increases.

The five themes I have focused on in this book are as follows:

1. Raising children successfully is not totally shaped by what parents do alone. It is much more of a **partnership** between parents, other people, and children themselves.

2. It is important to appreciate difference or **diversity** amongst individuals. We cannot and should not seek

to mould young people to be all alike, or to turn out exactly how we want them to be. This is not what good parenting is about.

3. Effective parenting comes about through **Positive parenting** methods that involve praise and encouragement and characterises the approach we should aspire to.

4. When trying to problem-solve difficulties in young people, we need to consider all the influences on young people. This is what I call, seeing the **"big picture"**.

5. Do not expect a smooth ride and instead **expect problems.** This is normal.

Let me say more about these key themes.

Partnership

The analogy of parenting with travel, which I described in the initial part of this Introduction, is a useful one because it illustrates the first key theme. If you take this on board, it is likely to transform your approach to, and satisfaction from, parenting. I know many parents are doomed to find parenting disappointing and stressful because of a simple belief: that they are *entirely* responsible for the way their children turn out. This belief is frequently reinforced by the attitudes and actions of others in society, who are quick to blame parents at every turn when young people present with problems. What should always be kept in mind is that children are products of biological, social, and psychological influences, which psychologists refer to as the Bio-Psycho-Social Model. You as a parent have a very important, but not an exclusive, contribution to make to your child's development. If you believe that your child is a blank page at birth, and it is entirely up to you to develop your child's character, personality, skills, and other aptitudes in whatever way you see fit, you will be forever disappointed. Parenting children is much more like a partnership with others, including your own child. The influences of others in society – friends, family, schools, and neighbourhoods are crucial, together with the way that your child sees and understands the world around him or her. Clearly, you will be able to control and influence some things but not others. The idea of partnership means that you need to see yourself as having a central, but not exclusive influence on your child's development. Although this takes some responsibility away from you, it actually makes the parenting task much more challenging. This is why above all, parenting is not always such a straightforward business. Seeking help and trying to develop your parenting skills should never be seen as a sign of failure but a sign of commitment.

I remember a long taxi ride several years ago, in which the driver outlined the difficulties he was having with his 14-year-old daughter. This scenario by the way is not unusual for a child psychologist, except in this case, I was more of a captive audience than usual. The parents were increasingly unhappy about their daughter's uncooperative and defiant behaviour at home. It turned out that she was a county level swimmer and this was at the root of the problems. The father in particular, had helped, encouraged, and supported his daughter's swimming over several years and now she was not showing any interest and was refusing to continue with the sport. He perfectly understood that the swimming involved great demands on her. She had to wake at 5.00 am every morning to do two hours swimming practice before school and then a further two hours each day after school. Each Saturday there was further swimming practice and more often than not, competitive swimming with her club. She wanted more time to do things with her friends, including boy friends, as well having more time to do schoolwork, the volume of which was gradually increasing. The poor man was completely devastated. He was feeling that she was letting herself down and that he had somehow failed to "keep her on track". He and she had always enjoyed a very close relationship and now this was now being threatened as well.

I don't know the outcome of this situation; I hope it worked out well. Parenting is a delicate balance between sound guidance and responding to a child's abilities and needs. No parent ever really gets this completely right all of the time. If there is a frequent mistake, it is that parents have a rigid view from the outset about what they expect of their children, before they have learned to know them as individuals. You may have ambitions for your child but they may not be appropriate for any number of reasons: - lack of skills, lack of motivation, competing interests and impairments such as social anxiety or learning difficulties.

Diversity
A further theme in this book is that of striving to see the value of diversity in people. No two people are the same and this applies to identical twins that may have identical genes, but

do not have identical emotions and behaviours. The fact that different people have different skills and abilities is probably the most significant feature of our species. It has enabled us to dominate (for good and bad), this planet of ours. If we value this quality in our species, we ought to see the value of diversity and difference in individuals, but we often don't. This simple failure can sometimes interfere with parenting and destroy family relationships. Parents often suffer because they have a fixed view about what are desirable qualities and can become unhappy if their child does not conform exactly to their ideals. It would be wonderful if every child were to be sociable, intelligent, determined, and emotionally stable, but this isn't the case and neither should it be. If you are able to value diversity and differences between individuals, this reduces intolerance not only within families, but also within societies. This is not to say that we should accept all aspects of human behaviour uncritically – we shouldn't, and we should strive to bring about change, where change is needed. A crucial aspect however, is the way change in individuals is bought about. We should avoid being pious and judgemental, rejecting and brutal. Instead, we can be objective, reasoned, and fair in helping individuals to change.

The way we view others is critical in how we manage our own behaviour and that of others. Valuing diversity and difference are crucial ingredients and from them flow a positive regard for others, which itself, is a vital component of effective parenting. Throughout my 25-year career as a clinical child psychologist, I have been impressed by the superb qualities of skill and character I see in the vast majority of parents. Also, there is not one single child I have ever met, who has not favourably impressed me in one way or another – this includes children and young people who have sexually abused others, been violent or extremely destructive. No child has ever struck me as "evil" to use an old concept. What I *do* see, frequently, is a kind of unbalanced state in many young people and adults. It is where their good qualities and skills become swamped or prevented from maturing by biological, psychological, or social circumstances. In some cases, this becomes a semi-permanent state and one can lose sight of what the person once was or could have become.

Positive Parenting

The third theme in the book is the value I place on positive parenting. This involves developing a positive attitude and techniques in helping young people to develop. Praise and encouragement are preferable to criticism and punishment. This is far more acceptable and effective for young people but also it makes parenting a much more satisfying end enjoyable experience. When young people are presenting with behavioural and mental health problems, quite frequently, they are suffering with low self-esteem as well. A useful aspect of positive parenting methods is that praise and encouragement do not make this problem worse, whereas punishment and criticism often do.

The Big Picture

The fourth theme of the **FOUR-STEP APPROACH** is a need to view child development in a multi-dimensional way and to appreciate all the influences on young people, particularly when problems occur. This means looking at all the influences on a child at a given time, as a way of understanding the nature of any problems. This is what I refer to as considering the "big picture". This often requires more time on the part of parents, but in the end, it will be repaid by quicker and longer lasting results. The value of doing this is frequently seen in my clinical practice. Take for example, the experience of Jenny:-

Jenny *was just 4 years of age and on the point of being expelled (Yes, it's true!) from Nursery School because of her throwing objects and hitting teachers when things didn't go her way. The background to this was that her Mum and Dad had separated some 6 months beforehand after years of bitter fighting and arguing. Jenny and her Mum had to move home 2 months later and Jenny had little contact with her Dad with whom she had a good relationship. Following the separation, her Mum became depressed, and as is often the case with depression, had less time for Jenny. The quality of that time was also poorer, given that she was becoming more emotionally distant and preoccupied with her own feelings, both made worse because of the complaints from the Nursery. Jenny had good reasons therefore to show anger. She had just lost (emotionally at least), both parents! Despite this, the problem wasn't obvious to her Mum or the Nursery school. The Nursery knew of the parental*

> *separation but, given that this was not a particularly unusual event in the lives of many of their children, did not see the significance of it.*

The fifth, and last theme, is to expect problems, crises, and worse. These are normal and to be expected. Things are *abnormal,* if raising your children occurs without major problems from time to time. This has to be, because there are no "owner manuals" issued for your child at birth and there are certainly no updates either. Effective parenting is more about getting it right occasionally, and at certain critical times, rather than being perfect parents all of the time. You will not always feel you are competent. Even the most effective parents doubt their actions and abilities from time to time. Expecting, and coping with problems in your relationships and dealing with your children in as thoughtful a way as possible should be the norm. Failure from time to time is usual, and not letting such episodes defeat or demoralise you is the desirable objective. In accepting this less than perfect picture and yet showing a willingness and determination to try, and try again, it sends out a powerful positive message to what will be the next generation of parents. It will help *your* children develop a realistic attitude, and effective approach to parenting, which is the essence of the **FOUR-STEP APPROACH**.

IS THE BOOK JUST FOR PARENTS?

I have developed **THE FOUR-STEP APPROACH** for parents and carers, whether they are struggling to help young people with mental health and behavioural problems, or simply trying to work at being good parents. I hope the book will also be of value to many other people, such as staff in the mental health professions, teachers, health visitors, school nurses, and social workers all of whom are involved from time to time, in helping to resolve behavioural or mental health problems in young people. Many of the ideas in the book are well understood by those in the business of helping parents and young people. What I hope will be of particular help however, is the *framework* for delivering therapeutic help and support. The Four-Steps are sequential ones, although I am not inclined to be overly rigid about the order of the first three steps. I do see it as essential, that the issues covered by the first three steps, are addressed before commencing Step 4 (Specific Techniques). My own experience suggests that the value and power of any specific techniques and strategies to change behaviour are greatly enhanced by first addressing the issues covered in the first three steps.

TERMINOLOGY

I have targeted the book primarily to address the parenting of young people up to 17 years of age, and use the term "young people" throughout, for this age range. I will be more specific at times, and refer to "children" for those of 11 years of age and below, and "adolescents" for those 12 years and older. When I need to be even more specific, I will use "infancy" for those under 3 years of age; "early childhood" for those between 3 and 5 years of age; "middle childhood" for those between 6 and 8 years of age, and "late childhood" for those between 9 and 11 years of age. "Early adolescence" covers those between 12 and 14 years of age and "older adolescence" refers to those between 15 and 17 years of age.

Throughout, I have tried to use gender-neutral terms such as "young people" and "children" unless I want to make a point that relates specifically to a male or female, in which case I will use one of those terms. More problematic, is when I use the word "parents". It is impossible to use all of the appropriate words for each given instance, but I use this word to include foster parents, step-parents, substitute parents, and other significant carers who may have major parenting responsibilities, if not all of the time, then some of the time. Many grandparents and older siblings take on this type of role, and many children in institutional care have parenting provided by other adults (carers).

SUMMARY

I hope by now I have set out the basic logic of the **Four-Step Approach**. In summary, the next chapters will cover the following:-

Step 1 - Parental attitudes and expectations

Few parents have received formal instruction in the theory of childrearing. Rather, we learn from our own childhood experiences, observe and learn from others, and draw on instinct and experience. All these sources are helpful, and the big task is to sort them out into a sensible set of attitudes and expectations about our children.

Step 2 - Parenting style

We learn much from our own early experiences and combine this with aspects of our own character and personality to develop a particular kind of parenting relationship with our children. Whist we all have our own individual styles, it is possible to recognise common themes and characteristics. Some are desirable, and form a template, which we should aspire to. Others are positively harmful, and should be avoided.

Step 3 - Social, physical and biological factors

This involves many components such as friends, schooling, neighbourhoods, religious/spiritual beliefs, physical health, and individual personality traits. Parents need to consider these things, in order to tailor their parenting and parenting beliefs to the needs of their child. This represents the Bio-Psycho-Social approach to understanding young people and is valid for an understanding of normal child development, as well as for when mental health and behavioural problems emerge.

Step 4 - Techniques and strategies

This very much represents practical parenting skills. Once you have a clear parenting direction underpinned with appropriate expectations and attitudes, you will at times need some techniques. This will be necessary given that most parents find that simply communicating their wishes to young people is not enough to bring about change. Psychologists over the years have developed a number of very powerful techniques from studies of why people, and other species for that matter, behave in certain ways. The most useful of these techniques is based on cognitive behavioural principles and social learning theory. The essence of both is to do with improving motivation in people to make changes in their behaviour and attitudes. Although sounding very grand, I have condensed down these principles into easily understood and implemented techniques.

STEP 1

PARENTAL ATTITUDES AND EXPECTATIONS

Developing appropriate attitudes and expectations is a tough aspect of parenting to get right. The shaping of these much depends on our own experiences of childhood, our personalities, and what we have learned and observed from how other parents think and behave. These things are all important, particularly so because it is these attitudes and expectations that are unique to each of us, and make our parenting behaviour characteristically different from that of other parents. A further reason for the unique qualities of parenting attitudes and expectations is that they are, ideally, moulded by the characteristic, and needs of our children. An appropriate set of attitudes and expectations can reasonably be thought of as a perfect blend of our own parenting aspirations, shaped by whom we are and what we have learned, dovetailing with the individual needs of our children. We need to get this aspect of parenting right so that our children grow up to be healthy, happy, and fulfilled adults. Get it wrong, and we will always be disappointed and, what's more, our children will know it. I do not intend this chapter to be a full training course on this issue, but have sought instead, to set out some key issues, which you might like to think about, so that you can develop a set of attitudes and expectations that will help, and assist you, as parents. Importantly, it will help you to promote a sense of well being in your children that in turn, will prevent psychological and behavioural problems developing.

NATURE and NURTURE

A New Understanding

One issue, which is a core one, is whether children are the products of the social environment and their upbringing, or whether they are born to develop in set ways. This is a controversial area, and one which still excites passionate debate.

My own view is that people are very much a product of both nature and nurture but until recently, I felt that there had been an overemphasis on the social influences on child development. This included a wide variety of aspects of development such as the bonding between mother and child, parental style, and the behaviour and interactions with other children and adults. A great influence was the thinking of psychodynamic therapists such as Freud which amazingly, still has great credibility, despite a century of scientific advance in our understanding of the brain, together with new insights from behavioural genetics and evolutionary psychology. A sad consequence of this has been a blame and guilt culture towards parents, mostly directed at mothers. In the recent past, for example, poor parenting has been blamed for causing schizophrenia and autism. Even now, I find parents come to me, feeling entirely responsible because their child presents with a behavioural or mental health problem.

There is still reluctance, on the part of many mental health and other professionals, to accept the role of genetic or biological influences; a view, which in my experience, very much runs against the intuitive beliefs of many parents. Any parent, who raises more than one child, soon becomes aware of significant temperamental and personality differences in the early childhood months, which, cannot convincingly, be explained by parenting, or other social influences. Parents can be reassured that research very much supports this common sense intuition with many personality, temperamental characteristics, and mental health problems, having a strong genetic basis. This is not to say, that a child's experiences in life are of no consequence, far from it. For example, a child may have a strong, demanding personality, which if appropriately channelled, will enable him or her, to be single minded, determined and ambitious, in a socially appropriate way. Conversely, if the same child is exposed to many inappropriate experiences and adverse life events, that strong personality, is at risk of being channelled into anti-social activities, such as aggressiveness and criminality.

Key point
The essence of good parenting is to help the young people maximise aspects of their personality, skills and behaviour, which are likely to be assets to their development and to try and help them minimise, cut-out or modify other traits which are likely to be unhelpful.

Temperamental Differences in early infancy and the influences on adulthood.

It is a rather compelling research finding, that infants display quite marked differences in temperament, some of which predict certain patterns of behaviour years later. The first, and very influential study, was by Thomas Chess and Birch published in 1968. Children, who at two years of age and under, had an irregular behavioural pattern, involving irregular sleep patterns, irritability, miserable mood and who coped less well with change, were the ones most likely to develop behavioural problems in childhood. In fact, over two thirds of children, with all four of these characteristics, developed significant behavioural problems in later childhood.

In a more recent study, Caspi and colleagues (2003,) studied 1000, three- year- old children who had five different types of temperament: Under-controlled, Inhibited, Confident, Reserved and Well-adjusted. Twenty-three years later, when the individuals were followed-up, these early temperamental styles strongly predicted adult personality.

Nature and parents in partnership

Why should so many behavioural, social and personality traits be genetically determined? Why doesn't Nature leave it entirely to us? I believe the answer lies in the value to our species of limiting to some extent how we as parents can influence some aspects of our children's development, and yet giving us the ability to influence other aspects. This is the character of the partnership between nature and nurture, but our state of knowledge is such, that we cannot be certain, at least for any individual child, how much is Nature's responsibility, how much is ours and how much is shared.

Allow me to speculate, by giving an example of why Nature may like to have a large degree of control over some things, at least. Imagine a situation in which we might be living at a time when there had been decades of wars, conflict and violence, to the extent that it had become a way of life. It might be sensible for parents to raise their children to be tough, suspicious, aggressive and able to handle themselves well in fights and conflicts, with others who were not family and friends. Three disadvantages spring to mind. One, it might serve only to prolong conflicts, with the people never developing the ability to cease being aggressive. Second, suppose war gave way to peace: children bought up to be aggressive and warlike, would be poorly equipped to conduct themselves as adults and cope with the changed world. Third, would we really want to live in a society dominated by individuals with aggressive tendencies? I suspect not.

Nature's influence on us takes into account that the world is a changing place both physically and socially, and ensures that we as a species are able to cope, no matter what those changes are. Take an example from the animal world. Chinese pandas will become extinct if areas of bamboo vegetation continue to decline under the pressure of human development. It would however, take far more than a simple environmental change to bring humans to extinction, because of our extraordinary capacity to adapt to change, and control and modify our physical environment.

A major point to keep in mind is that we ourselves are poor judges of what these physical and social changes might be. Because of this, I suspect that human evolution has worked in such a way, as to allow us as parents to contribute to shaping the way our children develop, but imposes strict limits on our freedom to do this. Nature doesn't trust us that much. This, I might add, is an area of conflict we are about to face, as we develop the ability to modify genes. This will bring us into confrontations with Nature in ways we have not experienced before.

Would we want to become more dominant than Nature?
Suppose for example, that we could choose to get rid of genes that produced a tendency to aggressiveness. It is likely that many prospective parents would opt for it. What would happen? Would we live in a more peaceful world with everyone cooperating well with one another? Unfortunately, I suspect that there would be significant disadvantages, illustrated by two possible types of scenario that come to mind. The first is that at some point, when the majority of individuals had no inclination to be aggressive, there would be individuals who would learn to take advantage of being aggressive for their own personal advantage. By bullying, cheating, and aggressing against others, they would get their own way and profit from it with very little resistance from others. Some parents might then, choose not to modify the aggressiveness gene, to give their offspring this very advantage. Second, suppose the world changed in some way. We might for example, be faced with the threat of war or terrorism. There might be some natural disaster, which changes the social order. In these types of situation, individuals with some degree of aggressiveness, may not only survive and cope better, but may assist all of

us to cope and survive. Do we really want to take the risk of tampering with genes that control and determine many basic human attributes that have proved their value over time?

Take another example to do with human intelligence. I was listening to a radio programme recently in which it was suggested that it would be no bad thing if, through modifying genes, we could increase intelligence. There was no disagreement on this point. I wondered though, if it would really be that desirable. As it is, human intelligence has increased naturally year by year anyway. We know this by major studies that have measured changes in IQ over several decades. This is not surprising, given that the continuing success of our species depends on our ability to master the social environment and physical world. The more we learn about the world, the more we need to know about it to continue to make progress. Nature probably selects individuals with the qualities to do this. The process is however, very gradual. It would be different if, overnight, all parents had the option of increasing their offspring's intelligence by 20 or 30 points at birth. I rather suspect that as this new super bright generation grew up, other problems would emerge. Would they be happy? I'm not sure, but I would worry that unless there was an instant change in technology at the same time, that removed all jobs that didn't require high intelligence, there might be many unhappy people in the world. Equally, there might be problems if other skills, such as emotional and social ones, were not enhanced at the same time.

Following the terrorist attacks on the World Trade Centre, New York, on September 11th 2001 and the tragic loss of life in the buildings and hijacked aircraft, there was a resurgence of the use of the word 'evil' to explain, or at least describe, the behaviour of the perpetrators. Psychologists have long been interested in the capacity of individuals to perpetrate such acts, particularly after the Nazi atrocities in World War II. The study by Stanley Milgram, described below, is a good illustration of this type of research.

TORTURERS AMONGST US

Stanley Milgram carried out what is now a classic work in experimental psychology, back in 1963, at Yale University. He was looking into the tendency of people to obey authority without question, such as that which seemed to have happened with the perpetrators of Nazi war atrocities. The basic experiment involved recruiting ordinary men to take part in an experiment, described as being about the effects of punishment on learning. The experimenter/instructor, a scientist in a grey lab coat, told the participants, to give the subject, a male strapped in a chair, an electric shock if he failed to learn a series of word pairs correctly. The shock was to start off mild (15-50 volts), but was to be increased in stages, to 435-450 volts if mistakes continued. In fact, the subject was an actor, who had been instructed to make mistakes, and to act in a set way, for each of the shock voltages chosen. For example, in one of the eighteen variations of this experiment conducted by Milgram, the actor was scripted to do the following. With fewer than 105 volts, he would make a little grunt; at 270 volts he would let out agonised screams; at 300 volts he would say that he no longer wanted to take part in the experiment and at 315 volts

> he would scream violently yelling that he wanted to withdraw. At over 330 volts, he became ominously silent. If the actor failed to give a response, the instructor told the participant/ trainer to regard this as a mistake, and administer a shock. The instructor would tend to give encouraging words to the participants, if they started to falter or hesitate.
>
> I don't know what you would be inclined to predict, but a group of 40 psychiatrists whom Milgram asked, predicted that fewer than 1% of the participants would administer the highest voltage. In fact, 62.5% of the participants delivered the maximum shock (450 volts). Further experiments, by the way, showed no difference between men and women. Other variations on the experiment seemed to show that such factors as the type of setting, being some distance away from the learner/actor, and having a person in an authority giving instructions, all helped the participants to become highly obedient. Milgram and others conclude that these were not abnormal people (some 636 participants took part in all experiments), but normal people in special circumstances that made legitimate what were horrific acts.

I think the consensus view that has emerged, is that most of us have a capacity for the most horrific acts, given the right (i.e. exceptional) circumstances. The likely reason for this is that the capacity for social dominance, violence and other forms of aggression, has been genetically selected for over the course of human history. These characteristics have, most probably, been needed for the successful propagation of our species. In other words, we are all carrying some baggage from the past that may, in any of us, from time to time, produce totally unreasonable and perhaps horrific behaviour. I have stated this because it is helpful for parents to see gross aberrations of behaviour in young people as not wicked or evil, but a failed struggle with dark forces which reside in all of us. For some individuals the struggle is more difficult, due to adverse life events and personality characteristics.

A genetic basis to criminality and aggressiveness

One of the most interesting research findings in recent years is that of a very strong link between antisocial and aggressive behaviour, and a low resting heart rate. This is true of children, adolescents, and adults. This has been the subject of an excellent review article by Adrian Raine (2002), and seems a very robust finding based on 25 separate studies over several countries. Moreover, the association does not seem to be due to other possible factors like height, weight, other psychological factors, and life circumstances. Even more intriguing, is that low resting heart rate is a highly heritable characteristic in the range of 65% to 82%, To put this figure in perspective, a 100% heritability figure would represent a characteristic totally transmitted by genetic means.

Why should this be? The best-fit theory is that a low resting heart rate is simply an indicator for a whole range of other characteristics, which give certain individuals a different physiology and through that, a different psychological make-up. A low resting heart rate is associated with what psycho-physiologists call, low levels of cognitive and autonomic arousal. In practical terms, this means that some individuals have, to put it simply, brain states that are under active. Linked to this, other nervous system functions such as hormonal, respiratory, and circulatory activity are also suboptimally aroused. As a result, they have a greater need for mental stimulus to achieve, for themselves, an optimal range of brain functioning. A further feature is that such individuals cope with fear and anxiety better. Of interest, is that several studies show that soldiers awarded for exceptional bravery and those involved in bomb disposal, also have low resting heart rates.

The net effect of this type of psycho-physiological make-up, is that such individuals, are at times, driven to seek higher levels of stimulus of all kinds: - verbal, visual, tactile, physical and cognitive. Not only that, but they have a tendency to be less easily stressed, and better able to cope with fear and anxiety. An important thing to remember, is that the vast majority of people, including me, I might add, with a low resting heart rate, do not turn out to be anti-social and aggressive. It is simply the case, that a high proportion of people with those tendencies do have this heart rate characteristic. The actual path in life an individual takes, may be heavily dependant on not only this, but other psychological aspects of their make-up together with social and physical factors and the way life-events unfold.

Respecting individual differences between people

Nature has ensured that as a species, we are endowed with a vast collection of talents and abilities, which provide us with the means to deal with the natural and social world. These talents are there to help us benefit from the natural resources of the world, as well as to deal with unexpected and unwelcome events, such as natural disasters and major social changes. These talents, contained within millions of individuals, are vital elements to the survival and success of our species. From this point of view, all individuals are valuable, and the diversity amongst individuals needs to be respected and encouraged. In addition to variations in intelligence, there are major biologically based personality types that differentiate individuals:

Extroversion- introversion,
Neuroticism-emotional stability: Agreeableness-irritability,
Openness to experience-lack of curiosity,
Sociability-lack of civility.

A problem is that some abilities and characteristics at certain times seem less valuable, and even unwelcome. Take for example aggressiveness, which may result from a combination of one or more of these aspects of personality. Some individuals may be more prone to develop this characteristic than others especially if they have had a social upbringing that values and promotes it. If the society in which these individuals are living values cooperation and peaceful ways of resolving problems, those individuals are likely to be viewed as antisocial misfits. Suppose that, suddenly, a war was to occur; such individuals may not only find a role, for example, as soldiers, but they may also become heroes, and be highly valued by the rest of society.

Robin is a good example of a boy who was a misfit throughout his childhood and adolescence, whom I saw over several years throughout this time, and then met him again, when he was 26 years of age. He was an intelligent lad who lacked concentration and got bored easily, which became a major problem for him, particularly at school. When many of his friends could just about cope with the most boring of lessons, Robin became disruptive, disturbed others, and failed to concentrate on his work. As a result, he did less well academically than he might have done. When he left school and started a College course in building, he had a variety of jobs until, with some help from an uncle, he set up in business, fitting replacement windows. This blossomed: Robin enjoyed the variety in the job, including not only the technical side of the work, but meeting customers and dealing with suppliers and employees. Boredom was a thing of the past; partly helped by the fact that few of the commissions lasted for more than three or four days. Robin appeared to have benefited from having a job with variety and one where his need for novelty and stimulus were a positive advantage for him. Robin had not changed as a person much, it's just that as he got older, he could make more choices and find work and interests that suited him.

Robin is typical of many people who have talents and abilities that are not used or valued in some situations, but can be in others. Winston Churchill was a poorly motivated student at school and had concentration difficulties. His adult life was characterised by an enormous range of interests and talents that few would have predicted in his childhood or adolescence. It can be argued that his very appetite for stimulus, wide variety of interests and a capacity to be bored easily, were significant positive driving forces. They had less value for him and others at school, but became valuable qualities later in life.

A genuine partnership with Nature

Nature allows us to modify and change some characteristics a lot, a little or not at all. We do not fully understand the complexities of this, but we can reasonably assume certain things. Those characteristics that are unchangeable are probably necessary for the long-term success of our species and are needed, if not all the time, then for some of the time. Not all individuals carry all, or even some of these characteristics but at any one time, enough individuals in the population will have them. Other characteristics need to be present in the population, but are heavily modifiable to take account of the changing social and physical world. Still others will need to be developed from scratch, with parents, other adults, and young people themselves, having total control over such developments. It is this complex mix of processes, shared by no other species, that has given us such tremendous creativity, resilience, and control.

Take a physical characteristic for example. The height of children is heavily genetically determined, and on average, a child's height will usually be the average of both of its parents' heights. If the child is malnourished during childhood, their height is likely to be less than might be expected, as predicted by parental height. Equally, if the child had an extremely nutritious diet, better than their parents had had, their eventual height might be well above the predictive level. There are limits to this though. A child who is the product of two parents, each 5' 6" tall, is unlikely, even with the best nutrition in the world, to grow to 6'6". The point is that there is scope to modify within limits what is genetically given, but this varies depending on the characteristic, and also varies in terms of how much we are able to modify particular characteristics.

> **Key Point**
> *Sound and effective parenting is about recognising those aspects of personality, temperament, and skills, which are most probably biologically, given. In other words, it's about giving due recognition to the unique, biologically given aspects of your child. The challenge then, is to work to strengthen those qualities, which are likely to serve your child well in life, and to change or modify others, that are likely to be less useful or harmful to themselves or others. This approach recognises the biological basis of many behavioural, emotional, and intellectual characteristics but also recognises that change and modification can take place. Some qualities are much less modifiable than others. Currently, we do not have sufficient knowledge to fully specify this, and so parents need to make this judgement based on their own knowledge and beliefs*

GENES AND MENTAL HEALTH PROBLEMS

An interesting research project, from which we are still gathering valuable information on the influences of genes on behaviour in young people, is the Virginia Twins Study in the USA. This involves approximately 1500 pairs of twins both identical (monozygotic) and non-identical (dyzygotic). The research method is based on the notion that if you have two sets of twins, one set identical and one non-identical, for the most part, each pair will experience a similar social and physical environment but only the identical pair of twins will have the same genes in common. If a defined problem such as Attention Deficit Hyperactivity Disorder (ADHD) is totally genetically determined, both twins who are identical are likely to have ADHD, whereas there will be no such relationship with the non-identical twin pair. If ADHD is the product of the environment, then ADHD can be expected to occur with the same frequency in identical, as well as non-identical pairs of twins. There are methodological problems with this type of research, but recent studies, including this one, have used reasonably sound research methodology and analyses. Eaves and colleagues (1997) reported high rates of heritability for a number of common child mental health disorders. Attention Deficit Hyperactivity Disorder has one of the largest, with a heritability estimate of approximately 70-75%. Other problems such as Anxiety, Depression and Behavioural Difficulties, appear to have moderate genetic influences of around 50%.

PARENTAL EXPECTATIONS

I try to spend some time with parents discussing their expectations for their children, both in the long-term and what they feel is 'normal' behaviour when they encounter particular parenting problems. These expectations are shaped by parents' own experiences of childhood, their skills, personalities, and beliefs. It is, I find, helpful for any parent to examine these elements.

Pat *in her own words had a bad childhood. Her parents had separated when she was 4 years of age. She was the oldest child, with her two sisters and one brother all having different fathers, with different levels and quality of contact from them. Pat had had no contact from her birth father and it was only when she was 14 years-of-age, that she met him and thereafter, only infrequently. Her mother had long episodes of depression and Pat and her siblings had several periods in foster or residential care with the Local Authority. Not surprisingly, money was always tight, but the worst aspect for Pat was coping with what she felt was a succession of step fathers, none of whom she really got on with and many of whom were hostile and rejecting.*

When I met her, Pat was a single parent with a 6-year-old daughter, Kylie who was frequently oppositional and prone to temper tantrums. One of the features to emerge was that Pat was often unable to say "no" to Kylie's demands. In discussing this with Pat, it seemed that one of her main parenting objectives was to give Kylie the kind of childhood that she herself had missed out on. She didn't like to refuse

> *Kylie any request, or chastise her in any way. If she did, she felt guilty and a bad mother. Kylie of course learned that she could have any thing she wanted, usually right away, and if not, a few temper tantrums and tears usually did the trick.*

Sometimes the childhood experiences of parents are such that they have very subtle effects on their parenting approach. The example of John and Denise is a common example in my clinic.

> **John and Denise** *were parents running a successful publishing business built up by hard work and determination. This had resulted in many stresses on family life and both felt that they wanted to avoid this for their children. Their emphasis was on academic achievement, particularly for James a capable 16-year-old boy of average intelligence, who was not working to his ability level at a very academic school. There were considerable conflicts at home between James and his parents over his lack of progress at school, disinclination to do homework and general lethargy. James was reacting to what was a central expectation of his parents. So important was academic success to them, that he felt he could never quite match their expectations. If James had a motto, it would probably have been, "Better not to try than to try and fail". He feared that he would never be quite good enough. James was not a boy who liked to study much. He was however, a very well liked by his peers, was sociable and very good at sport and, like his father, practical at subjects such as Computing and Design.*

These case examples illustrate that parents should not be afraid to have ambitions for their children but that these should:

- Take account of their children's personalities and abilities.
- Take account of the developmental needs of their children.
- Avoid overly correcting for, or compensating for, their own thwarted ambitions.

Let me say a little more about these points.

Taking account of children as individuals

Successful parenting is not about implementing a rigid set of techniques but using techniques in a way that takes account of the personalities, aptitudes, and temperament of children. Some children are, for example, more prone to anxiety and worry than average. Taking account of their needs will involve much more thought and planning than would be the case for other children. Greater care will, for example, be needed to ensure that they are not exposed to too much frightening material on television or through viewing videos. Equally, ensuring that they are well prepared for difficult and challenging experiences will avoid unnecessary upset and anxiety. Other children may have problems such as dyslexia which may make them prone to low self-esteem and will need a greater emphasis on reward based approaches rather than punishment, as a way of promoting compliance with parental wishes.

Taking account of developmental needs

A developmental perspective involves taking account of how young people change as they get older. This is a difficult area for parents to keep up with and I suspect few get the balance just right. No sooner have parents sorted out an understanding of the needs of a child at a given age, and formed a strategy, when its time to change it. A good illustration of this are issues to do with independence. When is the right time for a child to go to school unaccompanied, to cross the road by itself, or to spend money without consulting parents? For matters like this, I feel it is worth parents remembering that an important goal of parenting is to help children develop skills to enable them eventually to cope well as adults. Gradually acquiring self-help skills, therefore, is an important element in this process and parents have to learn to let go at times and give young people freedom and responsibility. At other times, they may need to rein back children from wanting to do things beyond their capabilities. Unfortunately for parents, there are no set ages when it is suddenly appropriate for a given child to take on a particular level of independence or not. Judgements need to be made continually as to when it is appropriate or not appropriate for an individual child to take on a particular increased level of independence. It is very difficult to get it just right all of the time and this often becomes the cause of tension between parents and young people. Young people will naturally want to challenge rules and push their luck. Parents must, however; try to be reasonable. Often compromises are possible, including little "trials" to see whether a young person can cope with, or handle, a particular situation responsibly.

Living your life through your children
Bringing up children for most parents is an immensely satisfying experience but for some parents, the satisfaction comes too much about achieving their own personal goals and ambitions through their children. There is a little of this in all parents but for some it is an overwhelming need. Children either react badly to this, or grow up with a feeling of un-fulfilment either personally, or because they have not matched their parents' expectations.

What to do now

If you are concerned about some aspect of your child's behaviour or emotional state, take a little time to think about some of the issues raised in Step 1 of **THE FOUR-STEP-APPROACH.** *Examine yourself and your psychological needs and ambitions in relation to childrearing. A key point, is to understand that children are people in their own right, and part of the joy of parenting is in discovering their personalities and abilities and then to assist in their discovering and developing these. Remember that they have only half your genes and only one eighth from any one grandparent. Furthermore, the sets of genes contributed by each parent are randomly assorted. This explains why siblings, unless they are identical twins and from the same egg, generally have different psychological, behavioural and physical characteristics. These differences then become further influenced, by the experiences of growing up. The excitement and joy of parenting should not be through raising mirror copies of yourself, or of creating children from some type of blueprint of your own making. The real joy is assisting in the development of unique individuals. There are a number of good books on this topic for further reading including The Seven Worst Things Parents Do by JC and LD Friel (1999)*

STEP 2

PARENTING STYLE

I know that 'Parenting Style' sounds like some type of designer parenting idea. You may half expect me to talk about how to tell little Gareth off with panache. Instead, I have to say, it refers to something a lot less glamorous but extremely important. Parenting style is more than just a technique of parenting, but the bedrock on which many other aspects of parenting are built. It is more of a philosophy of parenting and once you get this right, it is easier to know how to respond to any unexpected parenting issue as well as any persistent parenting problems. It is, though, a complex issue because it is tightly connected with a parent's own personality, emotional make-up and behavioural style.

There are several aspects to parenting style, but I have focused on those which I believe are the most important. The first aspect focuses on the ways all of us see and understand the world around us, including other people. Then I cover issues to do with attachment and bonding, simply because I feel this aspect, although important, is overemphasised and causes unnecessary anxiety to many parents. I then deal with issues to do with how parents talk and communicate with young people, followed by the importance of promoting independence. Finally, I address the major parenting styles that researchers have found helpful in analysing how key elements of parenting behaviour affects young people.

WAYS OF UNDERSTANDING PEOPLE AND THE WORLD

The trouble with human kind is that we have a tendency to simplify things and fit perceptions of events to known "templates". Forgive the psychological jargon, but perceptions refer to any way of taking in the world through vision, hearing, taste, smell, and touch. A template is a construct we have in our heads which affects the way we understand the world. If I am depressed, I will have a tendency to see things in a negative way, however good those things might be. Equally, if I am extremely happy, I may be inclined to see the world through 'rose tinted spectacles'. This tendency to simplify and see the world through mental constructs may be a bother at times, but there are undeniable advantages in it for us. The basis of this process is located at cellular level in the brain. Visual perception is a good example. The visual processing areas of the brain, known as the visual cortex, are at the rear with neuronal pathways linking it to the eyes. It does not work like a camera, either traditional or digital. Instead, some cells react to straight lines, others to horizontal ones, still others to depth and three dimension and others to colour. Unlike many other animals, we do not see things in the infrared spectrum or hear in the ultra-sonic range. Most importantly, in addition to this structured way of seeing, our brains have a strong tendency to interpret what we see based on, amongst other things, our past experiences and emotional states. I remember this being beautifully illustrated many years ago when, in an undergraduate psychology lecture, a photograph was projected on a large screen in front of thirty or forty of us and we were asked for opinions as to what it was. Our responses were many and varied but not one response was correct. We had been shown a photograph which had been copied from a newspaper, but then we saw the headline above it. It read "Loch Ness Monster Sighted". Yes of course, now we could all see the connection, but initially our perceptions of the image had been uninfluenced by the headline. Before we all saw it as a murky blob but as soon as we were given a construct, well it was obvious, wasn't it - or was it?

Our tendency to impose constructions on what we see is quite marked and applies to all our perceptions including the way we synthesise them into what we might call 'meaning constructs'. This actually is a fantastic evolutionary development with enormous benefits but occasionally, significant disadvantages. The great plus side to meaning constructs, is that they save us a great deal of brain processing power. Imagine how slow it would be, if we had to process everything we saw, heard, felt, smelt, and thought from scratch - with every single experience, every second of the day. We just could not do it. I for example, would be incapable of driving my car safely. I rely on my brain working on automatic for much of the time, using existing 8: the car control mechanics, the road conditions and the behaviour of other vehicles, pedestrians and so on. When the unexpected or unusual occurs, my brain knows (hopefully) when to switch off automatic processing and get me actively thinking and processing again; but even then, I will continue to rely on my existing templates and constructions. I have never for example, experienced an elephant flying through the air towards my car. If I were to, I would have no difficulty in making out what was happening. I would not have to have previously experienced this combination of events, but I could piece together knowledge and experience from the past to make appropriate judgements. I would have seen elephants before, know of the dangers of airborne hazards, and could even calculate the likely impact time, unless I took avoiding action.

This wonderful brain system has, however, occasional social disadvantages because we don't all see, think, feel, smell, touch and understand things in the same way. Some examples come to mind:-

- Sometimes two people will see the same event differently but it is not due to any differences in what each actually sees, but by differences in their emotional states and prior experience. A client of mine, a 12-year- old girl became extremely upset at the sight of light blue jeans. As you can imagine, this was the opposite reaction of most people, even allowing for the fact that, at the time, jeans were sliding out of fashion. Her stepfather, who frequently wore blue jeans, had persistently sexually abused this girl. She was seeing, as you will appreciate, more than just a pair of blue jeans.

- We frequently make errors when it comes to understanding other people's characteristics because of our reliance on templates and constructs. It has to be so, because if we did not rely on these, we simply could not cope with the enormous amount of social information that we have to deal with each day. For example, we may make an instant first judgement about a person's character from their physical appearance. This has adaptive value because in many situations, we simply have to make instant judgements. Our lives may be threatened, or we may have to act quickly to make a decision about how much we can trust a person - without much time to construct an extensive and reliable character profile. Of course, we frequently get it wrong, but in many situations there is a possibility of reappraising our judgement at some later point, as we obtain more information to work on.

- We can easily misconstrue the actions of others as well. Often, we have to draw conclusions about their actions quickly so that we know how to act. Most of the time we probably get it right but, at other times, mistakes occur and we may be then viewed by others as acting unreasonably, foolishly or badly. An aspect of this problem is that we often develop stable "templates" or stereotypes of how we perceive people, even applying them to strangers. "All men are bad", "Black people are not to be trusted", "Muslims are fanatical". It makes life a lot simpler, but has huge undesirable consequences for the well-being of societies and individuals.

So important a part of our daily lives is this need to evaluate the actions, thoughts, and feelings of others that it becomes an important part of our leisure activity: reading novels, watching TV soaps and films, buying socially oriented magazines: and so on. All help to entertain, but at the same time help us to develop useful skills in interacting with others. The trouble is that much of the media overworks the "template" idea. People are stereotyped, and characters often portrayed in extreme ways – good or bad, weak or strong, sensitive or insensitive, and so on.

All in a name

In a study to show how stereotypes play an important part in making social judgements, Adler, in an article in the New Scientist, quotes a study by Birmingham, who asked 464 psychiatrists to make a diagnosis of a 24 year old man (Matthew,) who had assaulted a train conductor. Half were provided with details of the man, but he was referred to as Wayne. The other half were given exactly the same details, but were told that the man's name was Matthew. 'Matthew' was generally believed to have mental health problems, notably schizophrenia, and was felt to be in need of professional help. 'Wayne' on the other hand, was more likely to be seen as a malingerer, substance abuser or suffering from a personality disorder. Most people it seems associated the name Wayne with undesirable characteristics. The name 'Matthew' on the other hand, clearly had positive connotations for the people questioned.

The reason for my discussing these issues of perceptions, constructs and templates, is that good parenting involves helping young people to develop skills to make social judgements, in as reliable a way as possible. Parents are powerful models for showing how to do this. Showing young people how to make social evaluations and judgements is an important task. A key challenge is to help young people to appreciate that we are all vulnerable to simplistic and stereotyped judgements. Even more importantly, it is getting over the message that we do not all have the same templates or stereotypes.

A more direct reason for understanding this tendency to stereotype is that it is a powerful influence on parenting behaviour. One notable pitfall is for parents to misconstrue the motives, feelings and attitudes of young people. Many parents, particularly in the early stages of their parenting careers, have little experience of children. Their templates are probably useful for interactions with, and the understanding of, adults but less useful with children. There is no easy answer for dealing with this, but I feel it is helpful if parents learn to be very cautious when trying to make interpretations of child behaviour.

ATTACHMENT

Infants and young children develop well, psychologically and socially, if they are able to develop close emotional and social relationships with others. Most commonly, this is the mother, but research suggests that other people, such as fathers, grandparents and older brothers and sisters, can equally well provide this. Some years ago, there was much made of attachment as a vital aspect of human development and some researchers suggested that children needed such close attachment opportunities, that it was unwise of mothers to go out to work in the first few years of the lives their children. The case, I think, was overstated, with the result that many mothers felt guilty about working outside the home. There was also criticism of children placed with other carers such as nursery nurses and nannies etc. Worse still, children who had been fostered or adopted, were often felt to have been psychologically damaged, and much of any problem behaviour they showed, became attributable to interruptions in maternal and other types of adult attachments. Much of the literature which bought this rather unhelpful view about, was based on human and animal studies that involved gross maternal *privation* (long term loss of the mother) - involving for example, children who had been separated from their mothers at an early age, and placed in orphanages and other types of institutions. Many researchers then extrapolated from this to claim that lesser degrees of inadequate maternal bonding or maternal *deprivation*, (short periods of separation) can have detrimental effects on young people.

The important thing with this issue is to keep a sense of proportion. Most children are very resilient and can cope with reasonable interruptions to maternal care. Children have a need for their feelings of safety and security to be attended to. If there is a need for any substitute care over short periods, the carers should be known to, and trusted by the child. Infants and young children, particularly under 5 years of age, ideally need enough opportunity to talk, laugh, play and engage in activities with one or more key adults who will remain an influence in their lives for several years. This enables them to develop warm, loving relationships and a sense of security, which in turn, helps them to have confidence enough to leave the carers to play with others and explore their surroundings etc. If successful, they will for, example, be able to make the transition to school without great amounts of separation anxiety, and develop friendships with other adults and children.

Infants develop attachments to a number of adults

The results of research by Schaffer & Emerson (1964) challenges the worst claims of those who make too much of the effects of interrupted mother-child attachments by showing that multiple attachments seem to be the rule, rather than the exception. They followed the development of 64 infants throughout their first year through to eighteen months of age. At seven months of age, 29% of infants had formed more than one attachment - with 10% forming five or more attachments. At 10 months of age, 59% had formed more than one attachment and by 18 months, this was true of 87%. At 18 months of age, 50% approximately, had the strongest attachment to mothers and 34%, the strongest attachment to fathers: about 17% had equal levels of attachment to both mothers and fathers.

POSITIVE AND NEGATIVE TALK

All of us like to hear positive things.
- "Well Done"
- "Thank You"
- "You are so Kind"
- "You are so thoughtful"

These words evoke warm, pleasant feelings, no matter who says them to us. They are even more powerful when spoken by people who are, in psychologists jargon, high status. For adults, that might be the boss or persons we love; for children, it may be parents, teachers and a wide range of other adults. All of us are 'programmed' to respond to this kind of talk through several millennia of evolution. These positive remarks are so highly valued that we often design our behaviour to elicit them. The basic reason for this is that we are social creatures who operate in families, tribes, groups, and nations. We cooperate with one another to achieve our own, and collective goals - even, I have to say, if it means at times, ganging up on others to achieve those goals.

It follows from this, that it is important to build positive remarks into your parenting vocabulary. This may at first, sound all too obvious given that most parents tend to remember to give approval for the unexpected or exceptional deed or thought produced by young people. The real challenge however, is to remember to do it *frequently* for the things you appreciate and approve of, even when these seem to be done automatically, day after day.

- "Thank you for walking the dog – It's great how you do it without being asked most days"
- "Thanks for being so good about getting up on time and getting yourself off to school every day this week"
- "Wow, your hair looks great again. How do you manage to do it so well day after day"?

Quite often, I'm frequently struck by how parents that I see rarely give praise, or say anything nice about their children. Some psychologists place a lot of value in observing this, and use it as an indicator of family dysfunction; attempts are made to measure what is called a 'lack of expressed warmth'. The value of this can be overstated, but it underscores an important point, that this is often a barometer of the emotional climate in the home.

It goes without saying, that negative and disapproving comments are best used sparingly, and then, only when necessary. Clearly, if Darren is in the habit of thumping his little sister most days, it would be unwise to say nothing, and wait for the one day when he doesn't do it and say, "Well done Darren for not hurting Melissa today". Actually, that strategy might well work over time – say several weeks; but in the meantime, Melissa is getting black and blue and is probably wondering what you intend doing about it. Darren needs verbally chastising for his actions along with some other measures. These will be outlined in **Step 4**.

> **Key Point**
> *Try to make a point of monitoring the expression of warm positive feelings by yourself to your child and to other members of your family. How about a minimum of at least one positive comment, or remark each day, to each person in the family!*

INDEPENDENCE

Successful parenting is in part, about helping young people to reach a stage at which, gradually, and over time, they can achieve emotional and economic independence. This in turn is the gateway to personal and social maturity for young people. The pace and quality of this has to be geared to the young person's needs. Some young people will achieve certain landmarks of independence quicker than average. Girls for example, tend to achieve independence and maturity much earlier than boys do. Many parents find that helping young people acquire independence is fraught with problems, and do not facilitate this. More often than not, this reticence arises from their own anxieties, rather than any lack of capacity in young people. Children of such parents tend to be over-protected from the everyday demands of life. The parents are all too willing to bend over backwards to accommodate their child's wishes and demands. I have seen many children who are so effectively over-protected, that they lag behind in social, behavioural, and emotional development. By late childhood, it then becomes a self-fulfilling prophecy - the children cannot cope with demands on them as effectively as most of their peers - and the parents' continue to step in ever more frequently, to help and assist. By middle to late adolescence, these children are unable to catch a bus, make a train journey, buy clothes by themselves, manage money and make and sustain relationships with others of the same age. For many, this should be the point at which they should be able to leave home for university, for example, but instead, are unable to make the transition.

There is of course, no rulebook or owners manual for parents to consult for any individual child. Instead, parents need constantly to adjust their parenting to permit and encourage the promotion of independence and with it, social and personal maturity.

> ***Key point***
> *Try to make the development of independence one of the cornerstones of your parenting approach. There should be satisfaction in seeing young people achieve key milestones in self-help skills and in doing beneficial things for themselves and others that months beforehand, they were unable do. What's more, they get a sense of achievement and you - a sense of satisfaction over this happening*

PARENTING STYLE

This is to parenting what personality is to a person. Get this right and so many other things will fall into place. For some time now, researchers have identified a number of types of parenting styles and how these styles are likely to influence young people. Peoples' parenting styles do not, of course, always fall into neat, discrete categories. Some people have styles that overlap one or more categories and, more commonly, have styles that vary from one day to another, or even within the same day. The categories are however, surprisingly recognizable, particularly in families functioning very well or very badly.

Authoritarian

An authoritarian parent is the sergeant major of the parenting world. They have rules that cannot easily be broken or modified and children are expected to obey them unquestioningly. Such parents do not tolerate much discussion or explain the reason behind their requests; after all, "rules are rules". Many authoritarian parents lack the ability to show emotional warmth but others can manage to incorporate some warmth into their style, which appears to have a less adverse effect on children as they grow up. This need for control, within a rule bound framework, is frequently achieved by the use of verbal and perhaps physical aggression. Shouting and other harsh verbal interactions characterise whole families and is a breeding ground for foul and offensive language within the family. There is a large element of fear as a control mechanism with this parenting style, backed up by punishments if there is rule breaking or non-compliance. Rules, demands and expectations are often quite arbitrary and almost wholly based on the preferences of parents, with no account taken of young peoples' wishes, skills or personality attributes.

- "Homework must be done as soon as you get back from school"
- "You must tidy your room every day"
- "You shouldn't have got yourself so dirty doing that"

The consequence of this is that young people gradually learn to give as good as they get. They bark back at parents, and become adept at turning rules to their own advantage. If an issue does not have a rule that covers it, their response will be to ignore whatever needs to be done. Remember, they haven't been bought up to use their initiative, but to follow rules and to do as they are told! There is no recognition of a need to use common sense - to anticipate - or do things without asking. This, of course, infuriates parents, who yell and shout, prescribe more rules and make more demands, as their authority is challenged and undermined. The authoritarian approach however, does get results; at least initially, but as young people get older, it gets harder for parents to make the approach work; forcing them to become even more punitive and rule bound. Then, as children get older (and bigger), they simply refuse to comply and become immune to sanctions and punishments. They much prefer to do what they want to do, than comply with parental demands and feel frustrated as a result.

This authoritarian style of parenting tends to have undesirable effects on children with two main types of outcome. The type of outcome relates, not just to the presence of authoritarianism, but also whether this is an emotionally cold, rejecting type, or one that has some emotional warmth.

Authoritarian, with warmth
Authoritarian parents who are able to show some warmth in the relationship certainly get obedience and compliance. The children however, tend to have little confidence and have low self-worth. They also tend to become overly dependent on their parents. After all, they have been told what to do for years; have not had to think for themselves, or develop skills in internalising rules – they are used to rules being given to them. They also tend to have little consideration for others.

Authoritarian with emotional coldness
Authoritarian parents, who are emotionally cold, and frequently hostile and aggressive to their children, tend to produce children who are oppositional and rebellious, particularly in adolescence. Such young people become determined never to submit to authority. This becomes a real problem in school as well as in the home. I have seen many examples of children whose work suffers at school, because they do not get on with certain teachers. It can be an opposition to teachers with an authoritarian style themselves or teachers whom the child believes make unreasonable demands on them.

Permissive

'Anything goes' might best describe this style, with parents allowing their children to do pretty much as they please. The parents tend to be overly accommodating to a child's needs and tend do too much for them - encouraging dependency, rather than independency. The parents fail to encourage children to meet the reasonable requests and expectations of others and give in too easily to the demands of their children, even unreasonable ones. The approach is often one of appealing to the child's goodwill, rather than working within a framework of reasonable standards and expectations. As with authoritarian parents, permissive parents can be either emotionally warm or emotionally cold.

Warm and Permissive

Parents who are warm and caring but overly permissive are at risk of raising children who have a very poor ability to motivate themselves, work to targets, take account of the needs of others, and develop good self-control. It is hard for these children to develop a sense of direction in life and work to long-term goals. They have a tendency to want short-term rewards for minimal effort rather than opt for tasks that yield rewards in the medium or long term. Young people used to having their own way at home, also tend to be unable to cope with the demands and expectations at school. This inevitably results in passive non-compliance at school. This takes the form of failing to meet work demands and in extreme cases, refusing to go to school at all. Despite these risks, children bought up under this parenting style are the least worse affected. I see them grow up generally to be decent people, usually at risk of not achieving their potential, but often sociable, easy going and not capable of causing much hurt to others.

Cold and permissive.

Children who have permissive parents, but who do not show warmth are a more high-risk group. Children subjected to this style are in reality, neglected children: they are left to get on with it. I often see such children in homes where parents have considerable problems themselves: – financial, social and mental health. Many are single parent households. Children in these households face real problems, the outcomes for whom are difficult to predict. The reasons for a poor outcome are probably not hard to understand. Such children will not have been used to appreciating that there are social rules and limits on unacceptable behaviour, as well as having poor parental models as to what constitutes desirable behaviour. They will not have been exposed to a feeling of being loved or wanted, or of being exposed to good role models for successful living. Ideally, children need to develop with appropriate limits and standards set by parents. Then, after time, children are able to start setting limits and standards on their own behaviour. Despite these risks, some children from cold permissive homes seem to rise from the ashes and achieve amazing things whilst others seem to struggle with life. The survivors of this type of parenting probably benefit from having a stable personality and a range of positive, naturally occurring skills. They learn very early on, that they are on their own and will have to work things out for themselves. They will often seek inspiration from other adults, either within the family or outside it. Many adults sense the need in these children and step in as substitute parents. Other, less fortunate children, may go the opposite way, and become replicas of their parents.

Authoritative Parenting

An authoritative parenting is the gold standard we should aim for. It is characterised by six key parenting qualities.

- A reasonably clear set of standards for the personal and social behaviour expected of young people
- A reasonably clear set of moral values
- A tendency to encourage, rather than dictate
- A tendency to be consistent in applying rules and in acknowledging appropriate behaviour
- A tendency to reasonableness in the setting out of standards of behaviour expected of young people
- An emotionally warm, supportive, and encouraging style

The difference between authoritative and authoritarian parents is that the standards set by authoritative parents are reasonable, justifiable, and consistent and conform to generally acceptable social values. The standards set by authoritarian parents are much more arbitrary - many based on personal whims. Authoritative parents are willing to explain decisions they make, and may enter into negotiations with young people, with compromise solutions often emerging. Where disagreements emerge, and compromise is not possible, parents understand that they exercise ultimate authority and are not afraid to exercise it.

Children bought up with this type of parenting tend to acquire the ability to be self-disciplined and self-reliant. This parenting style also promotes self-esteem and self-confidence. The reason for such a positive outcome is not too difficult to see. Young people benefit from clarity and consistency over what is expected of them. What standards and expectations there are, tend to be based on sound, justifiable principles. In other words, they will make sense to the young person, even if at another level, they may disagree with them. The consistency of approach, underpinned by clearly understood values, assists young people in what psychologists call the internalisation of values and standards of behaviour. This means that young people accept rules and standards of behaviour as their own as opposed to resenting them because others have imposed them. In time, young people can then anticipate and work out what to do for themselves, without being instructed by others. This results in fewer conflicts with parents and others and promotes early maturity. Young people also benefit from a reasonably warm emotional style, which is one of the hallmarks of this parenting style.

Yes, I know this all sounds laudable, but surely, you are thinking - too perfect to be achievable? Well yes, but note, I use the words 'reasonable' and 'tendency' throughout. It is a common misconception that *good* parenting is *perfect* parenting and that parents have to get everything right all of the time. My belief is that you do not have to be 100% consistent all of the time with an authoritative parenting style. This is in marked contrast to the authoritarian parent, who will expect perfection of themselves and their children, *all* of the time. It also contrasts with the permissive parent for whom this is not an important issue anyway. The great benefit authoritative parents have is that their approach is grounded in rationality. Because of this, their expectations of young people are predictable by the young people themselves and, therefore, parents do not have to define their wishes and expectations all of the time. What effective parents are able to do is to be aware of crucial times when they need to take the time and effort to spell out clearly what they expect of their children. These I like to define as 'key moments'. Furthermore, effective parents develop skills in knowing when key moments occur. I think it important to say more about this aspect of parenting quality.

KEY MOMENTS

What is a key moment? It sounds I know, like a romantic interlude but in reality, it's very practical and is one of the hallmarks of effective parenting. With key moments, you don't have to be a perfect parent all of the time – just at certain, occasional points in time. A key moment is very much an intuitive one when parents' sense that they need to make a stand over an issue where there is disagreement with their child; or that there is some principle or value which must be clearly defined.

Let me give an example, which might be true for any of us. At some point during childhood, 95% of children steal something. Given this high frequency, occasional episodes of stealing can almost be regarded as a normal part of child development.

When this happens, it takes most parents by surprise and they rarely have a well thought out response. They may have been at pains to point out that stealing is wrong and hopefully, will have demonstrated honesty themselves in their everyday lives. When knowledge of the theft occurs, it would be easy to over-react, under react, or deal with it in another inappropriate way, because you are busy with something else. Instead, if you recognise this is a key moment, you will want to engage as near perfect a parenting mode as possible. This means stating your disappointment, reiterating the moral case against stealing, and deciding on the most appropriate course of action. This might include returning the stolen items if possible - compensating the victim, together with imposing an appropriate punishment. It may be prudent to buy a little time by giving yourself time to think or discuss the matter with your partner, a friend, or relative. Clearly, this is a different order of response, requiring more thought and time, than many everyday matters where children break rules and disappoint.

Fortunately, for many more 'key moments' than given in this example, parents have more time in which to plan and act. This may be to clarify a moral principle, discuss an issue over which they have some concern, or take action where an agreed rule, or understood expectation, has been broken or ignored. For these occasions, it is as well to choose relaxed times in the home or during some recreational activity, to deal with the issues. Giving time and space this way can help to emphasise the importance of the event and make dealing with the issues, far less confrontational.

CONFLICTS OF PARENTING STYLES

***VICKI**, a single parent had become increasingly concerned about her son, Sam's tendency to hit his younger sister, Laura, whenever she annoyed him. This had been getting more frequent and more severe over the past few days and she was concerned that this problem would worsen. There were no current stressful or unusual life events going on, except that Sam had tended to be more demanding of his mother's time since Laura's birth four years ago. Sam was seven years of age and there had been an acrimonious parental separation two years ago. Laura could also be a little silly, and often seemed to delight in provoking Sam.*

Vicki had become aware that whenever Sam hit Laura, she would verbally chastise him, but this did not seem to be working, although he was remorseful afterwards.

After the family had finished their usual early evening meal together, Vicki announced that it was no longer acceptable for either child to hit the other. If for any reason, there was a dispute, she was to be called to settle it, wherever possible. Vicki went into all the reasons why she felt hitting and violence was unacceptable. To back up her point, she was able to cite how she has been hit by the children's father which the children, particularly Sam, had indeed witnessed.

Vicki said that she wanted to find a way to help both children get on better with each other and they all discussed ways in which this could be bought about. They agreed a reward based strategy using smiley face stickers, which could be

> *exchanged for a range of the children's favourite sweets, every 2 days. Each child could earn the stickers if there was no violence to one another during each morning, afternoon and evening period. In the event of one of them physically hitting another, there would be a punishment that would involve the perpetrator going out of the family room and staying in another room for 5 minutes.*

One of the biggest parenting problems I regularly encounter is where one parent has one type of parenting approach and the other has a different one. The most usual is where one parent has an authoritarian approach and the other a permissive approach. Believe me; this can result in parenting fireworks! You would not want to be in these homes! The 'tough' parent, most usually the father, tends to be over-controlling. The mother will then tend to try and 'soften' this approach, by being more permissive than she would usually be. She is driven by a concern, that her partner is being 'too tough' with the children. Unfortunately, the father, seeing the mother becoming 'too soft', then hardens his act even more, especially when the children start to exploit the differences between the parents. You know the kind of thing. Dad refuses to let Max go to a birthday party because he has been fighting with his younger brother that day. Max goes to Mum to appeal the decision. With a bit of luck, Mum doesn't know what Dad has said. Even if she does, Max can probably persuade her to overturn Dad's decision. Over the years, the parenting style gap between these two parents grows bigger, with each parent's style getting more and more extreme.

The sad thing is that several years down the line, both parents turn into the kind of parents they never wanted to be. Dad has turned into a great dictator and Mum, into a lovable parent, but one who is ineffective. Each of them becomes unhappy, and if the marriage has not already folded, it is at risk of doing so. This is not to say that each parent need be a clone of the other with exactly the same parenting style. It is important however, to work together in such a way, to avoid one parent undermining the other. The great thing about the authoritative approach is that it provides something for all parents and it accommodates differences in the personalities, values, and attitudes of a wide range of parents. The essential thing is to work together, and to be constantly striving to work together, to sort out any differences.

MARITAL ISSUES

Children seem to me to have an amazing sensitivity to any difficulty in a marital relationship. This is often despite parental efforts to conceal any problems. Most relationships experience problems from time to time – parents will disagree and argue which need not necessarily be a block to effective parenting. Some parents tell me that they, "never argue in front of the children". This is fine if you can do it, but I do not feel that this is an essential component of effective parenting. Disagreements are a normal part of any healthy relationship and arguments are almost inevitable. It does no harm for young people to be aware of the occasional difficulty between parents and more importantly, see how such differences are resolved or not resolved. It *does* become harmful if disagreements and arguments are frequent, perhaps on a daily basis. This will undoubtedly affect the emotional well-being of young people. This is even more true, if the relationship is characterised by bitterness and hostility between parents, and devastatingly so, if violence occurs as well. In most cases, children will have a reasonably secure relationship to each of the parents and so their sense of loyalty gets confused. If Mum attacks Dad, for example, does this mean that Dad is bad? If not, is Mum being unreasonable and mean?

Children see a fight between their parents as confusing in that it may challenge the beliefs they have about each parent, and in most cases, they cope by not thinking about it. At a deeper level though, it is emotionally unsettling. If the problems between parents are serious, young people start to detach themselves emotionally from one or both parents. When this happens, the authority of each parent is severely weakened. It does not matter how good your parenting style is, or how appropriate your parenting expectations are, they will be much less useful if your marriage is fundamentally flawed and this is evident to the children. I will say more about the issue of marriage in **STEP 3** but I stress it here, because of its importance in making or breaking attempts, to develop an effective parenting style.

What to do now

Try to identify what type of parenting style you have. It may conform to one of the types I have discussed or it could be a mixture. If there are major differences with your partner's style, you need to resolve them, and find some common ground based on the Authoritative parenting approach. If there are major differences between you, try to sort these out first. If it is too difficult, get help from trusted friends and family members, particularly when and if, you find it difficult to be objective about your current parenting style. Other people who know you, and whom you trust, should be encouraged to be honest with you. With older children of sufficient maturity, you can have family discussions to achieve the same outcome.

Do not try to be over ambitious and make too many changes, too quickly. This applies either to reconciling any differences between you, or to changing aspects of your child's behaviour.

*To achieve changes in children, pick one or two areas to target on which you can agree a strategy, and for which you feel there is a capacity for change in your child. Use the techniques suggested in **STEP 4** to help. Also, deliver the strategy in a framework consistent with the Authoritative parenting approach. This means discussing the options with your child, agreeing on the strategy, explaining why, as appropriate, but being firm about the need for a changed outcome.*

> *Finally, go for professional help if these steps fail.*
>
> *To put it bluntly, if you don't get this part right, don't even go onto **Step 4**. No technique can make up for a faulty parenting style.*

STEP 3

THE WORLD OF YOUNG PEOPLE

In this Step, I look at the many influences on young people – biological, psychological, and social. Some of these influences are unchangeable and beyond the scope of parents to alter them. Others are very much more subject to change to the extent that parents can incorporate them into their parenting strategies. Many parents fail to appreciate the significance of some of these influences on their children and, as a result, develop parenting styles that are inappropriate and doomed to failure. You don't have to be a child psychologist to understand these influences - they affect us all and we should know the basic issues. The key skill is to see them through the eyes of your child and understand how they affect your child

THE FAMILY

The family is probably the most important social influence on young people. The parenting style as outlined above is a crucial part of the family character, but another important ingredient is, of course, the composition of its members and the relationships between them. The family is very much in a state of change. Fewer and fewer children in the UK and many other western countries are being raised in families consisting of children, plus both birth parents, under one roof.

I believe that the easiest and the most reliable way to bring up children successfully is in the traditional two-parent family. This is however not always achievable and for some people, not particularly desirable. Two out of three of all marriages fail to work out despite, in most cases, the best efforts of those involved. Only approximately 50% of children now born in the UK will stay with both natural parents living together. Some parents have had such bad experiences in relationships, both as children or as adults, that they prefer to parent singly. Others are bereaved of a partner or spouse and increasingly, many serve as foster and adoptive parents either alone or with a partner who may or may not be of the same gender.

For most children in the UK who do not live with both birth parents, the challenge is to ensure that they have the benefit of the skills and love of both parents despite the fact that they may not be living in the same household. Sometimes this is not possible. I have met many mothers who have had such abusive experiences from their ex-partners that any form of contact with them is impossible to contemplate. More frequently, many separated parents hold such bitterness towards one another, even after separation, that they fail to be able to communicate with one another even if this involves making important, joint decisions about their child or children.

Parental Separation

Research findings suggest that when separations occur, a significant number of children are emotionally, badly affected. This is not to say that separation is necessarily a bad thing for either parents or children. If a marriage has gone horribly wrong, the hostility, and sometimes violence, can be very damaging psychologically for all family members. If this is the case, children may be emotionally better off with parents who are in two separate households. The research evidence does in fact support this.

The difficulties children face over parental separation are of several types - the four main ones being: the interruption of contact with one parent; the difficulty of managing their relationship with two adults living apart; dealing with feelings of guilt, and for many; adjusting to life in new households.

Reduced contact

The initial shock for a child is often the loss from the home of a parent, usually the father. The separation, for at least one of the parents, often comes as a welcome relief, but for the child, even if he or she has been aware of tensions in the marriage, the separation will often come as unexpected and unwelcome. It is also important to remember, that because parents haven't got on with one another, it doesn't mean that the same is true of the relationship between the child and their parents. It is more likely than not, that a child is emotionally well attached to *both* parents. It sounds an obvious truth, but many parents fail to see this and assume, that because their main priority is to sever links with their partner, it also their child's priority as well. Even if there is not such an assumption, some parents in my experience, try to engineer things, to hinder their child maintaining good contact with the other parent. In some cases, the reason is understandable, such as where there has been a history of violence and abuse in the relationship. Many parents then take the view that their child may be better off with no contact with the other parent for the child's sake or in the interests of their own psychological health. In such difficult cases, the Courts play a valuable role in arriving at a sensible contact programme (or not, if there are good reasons not to) taking into account parental wishes, together with, most importantly, the child's best interests.

For the majority of parents, the need will be for them to work together, perhaps with the help of the Courts, to arrive at a level of contact in the best interests of the child. Although difficult for the resident parent in particular, it will mean giving the child encouragement to visit the non-resident parent. Difficulties are often present when there has been an acrimonious break up and the child is aware that the resident parent, usually the mother, is unhappy. For the child, the idea of visiting Dad may seem like a betrayal of the mother. Another scenario is where the child is angry with one of the parents, usually the one who may have initiated the break-up, perhaps because of an affair with another person. The child, quite understandably, feels angry and may refuse to see the other parent if they are non-resident or want to live with the non-resident parent if they were not the instigators of the break-up. With these types of situation, it is important for parents to be patient and sympathetic to their child's difficulties. The child should be encouraged to work through the angry feelings. There will come a point when they can put these to one side and develop a new relationship with each parent, more so in the case of the non-resident one.

For most children, having reduced contact with one of their parents is the chief problem arising from parental separation. Research informs us that boys in particular, suffer most from the effect of parental separation given that they have reduced contact, or lose altogether, contact with their fathers. They thus lose the opportunity to grow up with a male model in the household with whom they can readily identify. The problem is of course, less acute for girls because usually they have their birth mothers at home. Parents need to work hard to try to keep up a good level of contact with the non-resident parent in particular, unless there are serious reasons for not doing so such as, for example, the threat of harm or abuse to the child or mother.

New relationships
When parents separate and live apart, it seems to me that the child's relationship with each parent changes. Two parents in the same household generate a different parenting style than each develops on their own. The behaviour of one or both parents, during and following separation and divorce, may change the perceptions and beliefs of children about their parents. A child, just like his or her parents, will need to make changes in their relationships with other family members

to make the changed family workable. The experiences of Gemma well illustrate some of the difficulties.

> **Gemma's** parents separated 18 months ago, when she was 9 years old, after her father had an extra marital affair with a woman (Laura) from his workplace. Father subsequently moved to live with Laura. Gemma is aware her Mum is still angry about the affair. She visits her father and has done so since the separation. She gets on well with her Dad and Laura and visits them at weekends, which also includes one overnight stay. She enjoys the visits, but what does she tell her Mum? If she has a good time and says so, wouldn't that upset her Mum? At first, Gemma used to tell her Mum that she hated visiting (although she didn't) then later, because Mum tried to argue that visits were bad for Laura, she kept quiet and now says very little about the visits.
>
> Gemma also has difficulty over what other things to tell or not tell her Mum. If she has a good time with her Dad and Laura, she feels that she can't tell Mum because it would upset her. Better to say nothing. Recently, her Dad told her that he and Laura were thinking of getting married when the divorce was finalised. She wouldn't dream of telling Mum this though.

The way to reduce the stresses on young people is to be encouraging of them to relate their experiences of contact with the other parent. They need to be given permission - to be told that some hurt might be felt at times, but that's what

Mums and Dads can cope with. If this is done well, young people can avoid the sense that their lives have become 'compartmentalized', and that every experience has to be weighed and evaluated to see whether the other parent can be told.

Parents who separate will also have a changed relationship with one another. One of the problems for children is that parents may retain or develop hostility and bitterness towards each other. Young people find this particularly difficult to cope with because in most cases, they are equally emotionally well attached to both parents. If one parent criticises the other (for whatever reason) in front of the child, the child struggles to cope with what or whom to believe. I often point out to parents, that it is the parent doing the criticism, who comes off worse. The child often views the critical parent as a person who is attacking someone they love. How would you feel in that situation?

> *Parents should try to work on their post-separation relationship to avoid open hostility and criticism in front of children. Even better, try to work at communicating effectively so as to be able to discuss such important, joint issues as contact arrangements, school issues and holidays etc.*

I'm often asked to recommend appropriate levels of contact between a child and the non-resident parent: there is however, no one solution that will fit all circumstances. Account needs to be taken of the child's wishes and the level of attachment they have already with a particular parent. Some children have an extremely close relationship with their father - perhaps stronger than that with their mother, If the father becomes non-resident, this situation might argue for a good level of contact with the father compared with a child that has rarely seen their father or who might have little emotional attachment to him.

A particular problem is when, after a parental separation, a child shows some resistance to visiting the non-resident parent. This might also be associated with showing emotional and behavioural disturbance after returning home following such a visit. This frequently causes great distress to the resident parent, usually the mother, who is torn between sending the child, and keeping him or her at home. Generally, I find myself trying to be reassuring and supportive over this. Very rarely is it the case that the father is abusing or ill-treating the child in some way, but many mothers understandably, conclude that this is the only explanation. More usually, children find coping with these forced changes very stressful. Particular problems arise if the father has developed a new relationship - more so if there are other children in the household. This can make it difficult for children to face the prospect of not only day contact, but in cases, overnight stays.

Further stresses on a young person can be the result of feeling that somehow, they are betraying a parent. If for example, they know that their mother and father are hostile to one another. It is difficult for a child to visit the non-resident parent and believe that this is acceptable to their mother. It is not surprising if the child demonstrates to their mother that they are unwilling to visit.

Another matter which I find takes parents by surprise is the fact that children also find the change *following* contact visits difficult to cope with. In many cases even if they have enjoyed the visit, it will have been stressful, at least in the first few months. There is the added stress of getting used to one household one day, then re-adjusting to another the next, often coinciding with a return to school following a weekend break. They will also have to get used to parents who now parent differently. Their parenting styles will change and there will be different rules and expectations in each household. This becomes even more complicated if new relationships have to be forged with new parental partners and any children they may have.

Al this argues for patience and tolerance between parents in helping a child cope with such major changes successfully. When it goes wrong, children can show signs of mild trauma and, as a result, develop a range of mental health problems.

Feelings of Guilt
Young people, particularly those below the age of 11 or 12 years, can easily develop feelings of guilt and self-blame over parental separations. This is often related to a developmental stage in middle to late childhood to egocentric or 'magical' thinking in which they see themselves in the centre of the world of events and as such, believe they have influence over them.

I remember a 9 year old boy, Joshua, who explained to me that when his parents decided to separate he could not work out why, but then felt that it must be because of something he had done. He remembered that before the split, there had been frequent rows between his parents. The atmosphere in the house had been tense. Joshua also tended to get into trouble with his parents, usually over non-compliant behaviour such as refusing to go to bed or not getting dressed on time. His parents hold told me that increasingly, Joshua had become the focus for a lot of parental tension in that they often argued about how to deal with him. He had gradually become another source of disagreement for them in the months that led up to the separation. It was therefore not too surprising that Joshua believed that it had been *his* behaviour that had caused the parental split. Both parents had been at pains to re-assure him that this was not the case but he still had difficulty in believing this. Part of his problem was that he loved each of his parents, so why did they not love each other?

However much parents reassure children on this issue, there is hard resistance from children to believe they are not to blame, particularly if the separation has not really made much sense to them in the first place. The way forward is to continue to stress that in no sense should they take any blame and reinforce this by honestly discussing the basic reasons for the separation.

Life in new households

It never ceases to amaze me just how well many children adapt to major life changes in a way that most adults would find traumatic. Others of course are less able to do this and for them, coping with life in new households is a particularly testing experience. Parental separation is usually accompanied by radically different living arrangements - a house move, a parent leaving, a new school, a new adult in the house and perhaps other children living in the same house as well. There might also be loss of contact with relatives including grandparents of the non-resident parent. I believe that most children could probably cope well with one or two of these changes. It is just that for many, they have to cope with *all* of them and quite often, in a short space of time.

For many parents, their choices of what to do after separation and/or divorce are very limited, and they and children have to make the best of it. Having said that, I'm often disturbed that many parents fail to see the possible impact of changes on their children and simply expect too much. This is rarely deliberate and probably happens because parents are pre-occupied with their own emotional, relationship and financial problems. The difference for parents though is, to a large extent, that they have the ability to make choices, whereas children do not. For example, choosing to live with a new partner and his or her children may be a positive choice for a parent but a negative one for a child. In many cases, they may have not met the person before let alone any of their children who might accompany them.

The thing to do wherever possible, is to spread out the changes. The options as far as any change of home is concerned, can be limited since there are often financial and legal constraints. If possible, it is best to have a breathing space after any such move before introducing new partners and their children, if they have any, into the house. Children need a great deal of emotional support through these changes. Parents, together with relatives and particularly grandparents, can not only help but also provide much needed continuity at a time of change.

The burden of information

One of the most common pitfalls is to burden a child too much with the problems surrounding separation and divorce. Children need to know the basic facts concerning changes, together with a reasonable explanation that is true, and at a level they can understand. Too often though, I come across children who are burdened with the emotional upset of a parent and holding too much information about the ins and outs of separation as well as financial and legal issues. This is not all due to parents being overly informative. It can arise from children who are very inquisitive and who make it their business to find out what's going on. Parents need to keep a check on this and 'control' the amount of information reaching young people. The basic thing to remember is that children can be psychologically harmed by being burdened with information and problems which they have no means of understanding or solving. Adults on the other hand can also find it difficult to cope with distressing news or emotional difficulties but choices are open to them and they have better problem solving skills by virtue of many more years of experience.

Some concluding thoughts

Parental separation and the aftermath is one of the most stressful life events for young people and their families. It's often struck me that despite the frequency with which this happens, we are generally ill equipped to deal with it.

In some ways though, perhaps such difficulties are not too surprising. When we are young, we naturally entertain ideas of what type of personal relationships and style of family life we aspire to. There are idealised examples in popular culture about ideal loving relationships and family units, which we are commonly exposed to. We generate ideas of what we need to do to express love to our partners and our children. Few of us ever give much thought to when things go wrong and how we might deal with events then. When we need to, there is so little time to sort things out and this is often at a time of great emotional stress for all those involved. This is where the help of other people such as friends and relatives is crucial. It is beholden on all of us to offer help to those we know who are going through these events. It is sometimes tempting to take sides. Let's all accept that separation is a fact of modern life (at least for now) and help those who are going through it in an uncritical and supportive way.

Marital Relationships

An important influence in forming the emotional climate in the home is the quality of the marital relationship. A few, fortunate couples, achieve a harmonious and loving relationship that can last through the years of child rearing and beyond. The majority however comprise a "good average" in which the marriage is a partnership providing mutual emotional support, companionship and shared goals. There will be the some disagreements and conflicts, occasionally even physical, but overall a reasonably supportive and satisfying marital state is cultivated. Less fortunate couples may have a relationship characterised by discord, bitterness, hostility, and perhaps physical and verbal aggression. We know from research findings that these marriages have a bad effect on children, often generating emotional, behavioural and other mental health problems.

The evidence suggests that bad marriages are not particularly healthy for children but we also know that separations and divorce can bring about a completely new set of problems. There is no answer to suit every situation but it is clear that parents need to evaluate carefully their marital relationship. If it is in a mess, it is likely to undermine all of the parenting strategies suggested here, given that consistency of approach, providing models of appropriate behaviour and reaching agreements on parenting strategies are all key elements of effective parenting.

Key Point
Take a close look at your marriage particularly if it is characterised by persistent hostility, bitterness, and violence. Can you mend it, either through your own efforts or with the help of friends, family, church or professional help? If not, you may need to consider separation

MARITAL VIOLENCE DAMAGES THE INTELLIGENCE OF CHILDREN

Whilst we have long known that children's' mental health is at risk when the marital relationship is poor and involves persistent hostility and aggression, recent research by Terrie Moffitt and colleagues in the UK (Moffitt, 2003) suggests the effects are so damaging as to affect the development of intelligence in children. The team studied 1116 pairs of twins, all 5 years of age and found that the mothers of 476 pairs had experienced marital violence and of these, 151 had experienced quite serious violence. This involved incidents such as being pushed, grabbed, kicked, bitten, hit with a fist, slapped, or threatened with a knife, thrown object or gun. Children whose mothers reported no such violence had an average IQ of 100 - the average for the whole child population. The children of mothers who had experienced violence had an average IQ of 92 enough to have an adverse effect on learning ability as these children were about to, or had already started their primary school education. The design of the study suggests that this low IQ was not the result of genetic influences, such as inherited parental intelligence, or differences in other aspects of the home circumstances but a result only related to the marital violence. It is not known if these effects are permanent but the authors believe that domestic violence increases the stress on children, which in turn impairs brain development.

School

School for most children is an important aspect of their lives and its importance is increasing. Children start primary school as they approach five years of age and most undertake pre-school education as well. In the last century and in this one, particularly since the 1950's, there has been a marked trend for children to spend longer in education. The number of 18 year olds in higher education in the UK has risen from 8% in 1970 to 38% in 2002 and is still rising. Add to this the trend towards postgraduate education, and we have a situation in which young people are in a much longer period of financial dependency on parents with many not being financially independent until their mid-twenties. This extends the time span for active, practical parenting and leads to schools, colleges, and universities having a greater influence and interest in young people.

The positives

For most, schools are a great place to learn about the world, develop social skills, make friends, and develop a sense of self-worth and well-being. I doubt that this is a controversial view and so I will not spend too long developing it. The relationship you have with the staff of your child's school is likely to be one of the key partnerships you form in your parenting career. Time spent developing the relationship, including choosing the right school, will prove well worth the time and effort. One of the problems for most parents is that in choosing a school, if a choice is available, it is difficult to predict what the educational and social climate will be like. Getting advice from friends and neighbours, visiting the school and looking at any performance league tables will all be of help but nothing will guarantee a good educational and social experience for your child. It is therefore important for parents to keep the school experience constantly under review. A good relationship should be cultivated with school staff and children should be encouraged to discuss their experiences and problems with you on a daily basis.

I feel that parents and teachers should be aiming to build on a child's strengths and be supportive in respect of his or her weaknesses. Strengths and weaknesses can be in any area of human temperament and achievement including common ones such as academic, social, musical, sporting, artistic, and technical. An important aspect of parenting and teaching is to take steps to identify strengths and weakness in skills and aptitudes. From a practical point of view, this will mean encouraging children to try new interests and activities but not being overly disappointed if they don't like them or show any significant strength in them. They may have to try 10 activities or interests before finding one that appeals. Even then, the interest may be short lived, despite encouragement. In addition to identifying strengths, weaknesses relative to those of peers may also be identified. At school, many areas of weakness cannot be ignored since these may be, for example, core skills such as reading, maths and writing or form part of the nationally prescribed curriculum. The aim here should be to support the child to achieve a reasonable standard of work, which is within their competence, but not expect them necessarily to excel in the area.

The negatives

School does not suit all children equally. In many ways, it is quite a demanding environment. There are considerable social and work pressures, which are unrelenting for much of the day. Most children not only cope reasonably well, but it provides for them, a positive experience. Others are less fortunate and school can quickly turn into a miserable ordeal. This can be due to a number of factors particularly where there are temperamental, mental, or physical health difficulties. I will refer to a few of the more common problem areas to illustrate how school is far from a uniform experience for a significant number of pupils. At this point, I should add, that just because I am spending more time discussing the negative rather than the positive aspects of school doesn't mean I don't approve of school or see it as a threat to children. The vast majority of children benefit considerably from their time at school but some are vulnerable to difficulties. The following comments are particularly related to the more vulnerable children, and how you, as parents, need to be vigilant and ready to help.

Anxiety

One of the most common problems is where children are temperamentally anxious. This often first appears on their first attending nursery or primary school and not being able to separate from parents easily. Children with marked problems at this stage may have problems later on in coping with school, particularly at so-called transitional points, such as changing classes/ teachers in primary school or moving to a new school. Some children are naturally more prone to worry than others and require very sympathetic handling. There is value in gradually getting such children used to being on their own and being in the company of others in the pre-school years. This should be done gradually at first with a parent nearby but then, encouraging the child to play at some distance from the parent. Mothers and Toddlers Groups and Kindergartens are ideal for this. Part-time attendance at primary school leading to full-time attendance usually follows and is usually sufficient to help all but the most anxious children. At other transitional points, it is helpful to prepare the child or teenager well in advance. It is common for most secondary schools to arrange visits to their schools for prospective pupils for one or two days in the term before the new academic year starts. It is helpful for staff to be aware of any particular difficulties your child may have so that their progress can be monitored and assisted.

> **Michael,** who was 11 years of age, had difficulty starting at nursery school at 3 years of age. He became extremely distressed and cried constantly when his mother attempted to leave him. She stayed with him on several days and then, on the advice of the Nursery staff, started to leave him after first settling him in. He still cried but within minutes, became calm and was fine for the rest of the morning. Michael gradually showed no upset on being left and all was well until starting full-time school. He didn't want to go on the first and many subsequent days and had disturbed sleep most weekends prior to the school week starting. This pattern persisted for several weeks but eventually he seemed more accepting.

There were further occasions when the pattern flared up again. These times tended to be when he had experienced some upset in class: - a teacher "telling him off", a temporary teacher taking the class or changes of class teacher at the start of each school year. There was one year when he took a dislike to one particular class teacher and the whole year proved a struggle to get him to attend. The major difficulty started when he was due to move on to secondary (comprehensive) school. He refused to go despite having visited the school with his class for a half day, then a full day, several weeks previously when all seemed fine. He was persuaded to try going into school but nstead of going into the classroom, he worked in the learning support base. He did this once and then refused to try again. Michael's problems arose from a tendency to excessive worry diagnosed as a Generalised Anxiety Disorder. His mother had a similar personality trait that helped her understand Michael's problems. A focus of Michael's worries was separating from his mother, coupled with social fears within school. These tended to be about feeling conspicuous in crowded places and being afraid of "standing out". He had problems in speaking out in class, walking into a classroom on his own and coping with unfamiliar people. It took several months of patient work, building up his attendance week by week, to help Michael gain enough confidence to attend reliably. School is far from being his favourite place; each day posses a challenge for him and there are some days when he is still reluctant to attend.

Bullying

Bullying is unfortunately widespread with up to 30% of children in the UK reporting being victims at one time or another. Of course, for every victim there is a perpetrator and some children both bully and are bullied. Parents need to be vigilant and be prepared to intervene whether their child is a victim, bully or both. It is worth stressing that bullying can be physical, verbal, and social. Social methods of bullying are particularly subtle and involve children being deliberately excluded from group and other social activities as a way of inflicting emotional hurt. Some bullying is transitory and in other cases, it is persistent. The best way to tackle bullying is by the school having a comprehensive policy. This includes education about the moral aspects of conduct between pupils, the establishment of rules of conduct between pupils (what's appropriate and what isn't), and the encouragement of incident reporting by victims and observers. A clear policy needs to be set out on what sanctions will be employed against pupils found to have been bullying so that perpetrators know what to expect if they are caught or reported. Parents can help by knowing what the bullying policy is and encouraging their children to report incidents in line with the policy. Action may also need to be taken if schools don't have a policy, have a poor one or are not implementing it reliably. Most of all, you should regularly discuss the issue of bullying with your child and monitor if it is occurring. Don't forget, your child may also be bullying others.

Learning difficulties

Some children have a generalised delay of their intellectual ability compared with others. If severe enough, placing them in the lowest 1 percent of the ability range, they are described as having a learning *disability* in the sense that they will struggle to cope with everyday demands without support and even in adulthood will require the help and support of others. Many more children have difficulties with one or more aspects of their cognitive (thinking) skills relative to their other skills. These are called learning *difficulties.* Some are reasonably easy to identify such as dyslexia resulting in difficulties in acquiring reading skills that can't be accounted for by a child's general level of intelligence. Others are more difficult to identify and pretty much cover all the components of cognitive ability. Some children have a poor memory for recently received verbal (spoken) information. Others have difficulty with memory for perceptual information such as maps and diagrams. One of the more handicapping problems is a difficulty with some aspects of verbal information written or spoken, heard or read. Such difficulties are often very subtle and require expert assessment to identify them and later, to remediate them. Most children with learning disabilities and difficulties will require specialist help and this is most likely to be recommended at the time of any assessment by educational or clinical psychologists.

An important role for parents is to be alert to any type of learning difficulty. Not all children will develop at the same pace and so don't expect your child necessarily, to be on a par with others of the same age. You need to notice if your child is showing a disparity in one aspect of their learning skills compared to others. Children who have dyslexia for example, first come to the attention of parents and teachers when they are slow to develop reading skills but seem to be doing well with other types of learning in other subjects, usually non-verbal, such as maths, art, music and sport.

Motor Skills Difficulties

A number of children have difficulty with some aspects of movement. Two main areas can be affected; fine and gross motor skills. Fine motor skills involve manipulative skills such as writing and other related types of hand movements. Gross motor skills involve whole body or limb activities. Children with serious motor delays of either or both types may have a disorder known as dyspraxia. In practical terms, children with marked motor skills difficulties find it frustrating to do basic activities that many of their peers can do with apparent ease. The act of writing can involve considerable frustration. Usually writing is poorly formed and if they try and produce better formed, more legible writing, they pay the cost by producing work at a much slower pace. This is, of course, equally frustrating. Similarly, young people with gross motor skills difficulties frequently find it difficult to play with their friends. Simple ball games and other activities involving hand-eye coordination can prove difficult and unsatisfying. The problems intensify with curricular activities at school including PE and games.

Activity based interactions are hugely important for young people in that they are important in developing social skills and friendships. In both primary and secondary schools, prowess at games often has more kudos than academic ability. It is easy to appreciate, therefore, why children with motor skills difficulties and disorders can have their enjoyment of school seriously affected.

Motor skills problems require specialist assessments by paediatricians, psychologists, or occupational therapists. Problems may first be identified in the first few years of primary school. As with learning difficulties, the comparison is not just with others of the same age but also with the child's other skills and abilities. This may be evident in a delay of developing the ability to ride a cycle, poor hand-eye coordination skills, and a tendency to be clumsy and accident-prone. Professional guidance is essential after a diagnosis has been made. Parents and school staff then have an invaluable role in assisting the young person strengthen their motor skills through patient support and appropriate exercises. As with so many remedial strategies, it is essential to make them enjoyable. Encouraging children to take up particular games and social activities where the motor abilities are not the prime focus but are a secondary aspect, can often accomplish this.

<u>Social relationships</u>
Although school can be a place for promoting social competence and skills for some children, it can be difficult for some to cope with these demands. Children with quite severe difficulties of socializing may have specific disorders such as Autism or Asperger's syndrome. Many more children have less severe difficulties but sufficiently severe to cause considerable stress. For some, the problem may be one of social immaturity that might be part of a wider problem of

developmental delay. In most cases though, it is a specific problem in which the child talks, acts and thinks in a way that is more similar to younger children. This does not occur all the time but more usually in specific social situations, particularly those involving new people at one extreme and at the other, those with whom the child feels comfortable. This frequently affects the child's ability to make and keep same age friends and instead, he/she is much more likely to prefer to play with children younger than themselves. Generally, most children grow out this and by the early to mid- teens, they have 'caught up'.

Other children have more difficult and persistent problems. It is not so much a developmental lag but more a specific difficulty that can be thought of as an impairment of personality or temperament.

***ASPERGER'S DISORDER.** This is a significant mental health and developmental disorder affecting between 36 and 71 in every 10,000 people according to best estimates (Frombonne, 2003). Many more children have lesser levels of difficulty, but do not fully meet the diagnostic criteria. The key feature is a basic difficulty in understanding the thoughts, feelings, and motives of other people. Young people with this difficulty tend to believe that other people think and feel like them rather than having separate thoughts and feelings. They also may have a tendency to be less good at reading emotional states of others through non-verbal signs such as facial expressions* *and body language. In practical terms, this causes young people a number of difficulties. One problem is a tendency to become excessively angry when offended or upset by others. The young person simply finds it difficult to see an issue from another person's point of view. The line of thinking goes something like, "If I'm upset because of what X has done, X must be in the wrong. Why else would I be upset". The difficulty often comes out in play with others in another form, typically with this type of reasoning, for example. "I want to play cops and robbers and I want to be the chief cop. The others want to be the chief cop as well but they are just being unfair." The problem is being unable to see that the other children may have their own wishes independent of what he or she may believe. This can often lead to aggressiveness, which exacerbates relationship difficulties even more.*

Another common problem is being excessively upset and distressed when other people do not do as they have promised, or said they would do. Again, the difficulty arises because they are unable to appreciate that there may be good reasons for this. As you can appreciate, others often see this as the young person being self-centred and selfish. This again leads to even more social difficulties. It is wrong to think of this type of problem as representing defectiveness in moral development or a character weakness. It is just one more type of cognitive difficulty. Don't misunderstand me, there are certainly people around with delayed or defective moral development but there are others reasons for this, and such people are far less frequently encountered.

An important way of helping young people who lack social competence is to teach them how interpret social situations. For most of us, this skill comes naturally, but for many young people, they need teaching. As a parent, you might note that your child has responded inappropriately to something someone has said. They may say something insensitive to another person. They may misinterpret the thoughts, feelings, and actions of others. These and many similar difficulties may be observed several times a day but many others will not be observed at all, given that you can't always be with them. You will need to point out gently the alternatives as well as explaining why any alternative would have been more appropriate. "Yes that man did indeed have a big nose, but in pointing that out to me in a loud voice, the man heard you. If you overheard someone say that about you, how would you feel"?

NEIGHBOURHOODS

Family peers and schools are important social influences on children but so too are neighbourhoods. This is yet another illustration of the idea of parenting being very much a partnership with others. To a large extent, other aspects of these social partnerships, such as those within the family as well as peer and school relationships, can be modified and changed to promote good behavioural and emotional adjustment in young people. This is perhaps less true with the wider set of relationships and social contacts that occur in neighbourhoods but even so, I think that there is an enormous pool of good influence waiting to be tapped, although there are obvious dangers as well. Let us first consider the benefits

Formal relationships

Sometimes contact with other adults is made possible through a wide range of voluntary organizations - some international like the Scouts, but many others being more local, often run by voluntary organizations, civic bodies and religious groups. There are also a wide variety of sporting and recreational groups offering team and individual sports. Aside from the direct value to young people of participating in such groups and gaining valuable skills, they have an opportunity to get to know other adults who are in a different role from other adults they are familiar with, including extended family members, family friends, and teachers. In my experience, most of the adults running activities for young people are extremely dedicated, many of whom give up huge amounts of their leisure time voluntarily to provide young people with worthwhile skills and experiences. These are, by any standards, good people to get to know.

Most of the leaders and organizers have developed good skills at interacting with young people and in most cases, they will have been vetted by the employing organization, including criminal records checks, as being suitable to work with children. They also have to be good at what they do or attendance just falls off. In most cases, the groups have a structure and rules are important if the activities are not to become chaotic and dangerous. This type of environment gives young people an experience of structured social activities outside of their normal social and educational environment. It also offers an experience of other adults, with whom they have a different kind of relationship, which is not as formal as with schoolteachers, nor as predictable and safe as that with family members.

Informal relationships

Equally beneficial, but perhaps in a less predictable way, are relationships that young people can build up with other adults in the neighbourhood who may or may not be existing family friends. One plus point to such relationships is that they may put children in touch with a wide age range of adults. Many older retired people and others whose children have "flown the nest", welcome contact. They have experience of bringing up their own children as well as time, which is in short supply for many parents. Young people may benefit by having wise and friendly adults who are outside the immediate family to confide in and get to know. The parent or parents of a young person's friend may also provide a good relationship as do friends or neighbours of parents. All of these relationships may become particularly important if there is upheaval and disruption in the child's own family.

In general, the more opportunity young people have of developing relationships with adults of different types and in different settings, the more it will help them develop social skills and a deeper understanding of people. This will add to the positive experiences of family, peer relationships, and school life. It probably goes without saying that parents need to monitor these relationships. There are people, even in well-known organisations who may abuse children. Despite these dangers, I think there is a greater risk of overprotecting children.

The downsides

In my clinical practice, I find that a greater issue for parents is the negative rather than the positive influences of neighbourhoods on young people. The worry tends to be that bad influences cause or contribute to behavioural and other problems. Andrew's experience well illustrates some of the issues.

> ***Andrew's*** *mother came to see me because unknown to her, he had been skipping school for a number of months. This often took the form of going in for class registration but then leaving the premises. She found out that he had been doing this with other boys and that all were meeting at one of the other boy's homes (the parents were not in during the day) and were smoking cannabis and more recently, abusing solvents. Things came to a head when Andrew and three other boys had been caught stealing goods from a shop resulting in a formal police caution for Andrew, given that this was his first offence.*
>
> *Andrew, who was 14 years of age, had for some years been reluctant to attend school, and only did so to be with his 'mates'. He had an average level of intelligence and no specific learning problem. He was the only child and living with both birth parents. Andrew told me about his peer relationships and increasingly, it became clear that these*

were very important to him. He was not a leader in the group but was heavily influenced by the others, most of whom were older with a history of truanting from school. He seemed to have few accomplishments, and not surprisingly, a low sense of self-worth. As I spoke to him, it became clear that being with his 'mates' was a source of great pleasure for him, irrespective of what they got up to. He opposed any suggestion by his parents that he ceased having contact with them. The school staff had been supportive but as the truanting persisted, they were finding it difficult to argue against legal action, being threatened by the education authorities, against the parents.

Andrew's parent's had tried several strategies to get him to attend school reliably and also to try and regulate contact with his friends, who they felt were a bad influence on him. Their efforts only seemed to make Andrew more resentful and angry and even more determined to be with his friends Before they saw me, they had taken the decision to move from the neighbourhood that would involve a change of school for Andrew . This in my experience is a risky option but it worked out well for him. I saw Andrew for several individual sessions after the move had taken place, primarily to work on improving his self-esteem. Staff at his new school also helped him by making determined efforts to engage him socially and educationally. I saw him and his parents two years later and learned that he had done well in his GCSE examinations and was intending to go to a college to study catering.

Many parents are in no position financially, or because of family ties, to move neighbourhoods. Parents need to keep a watching brief over the company young people keep. The best strategy is to help children develop good relationships at the outset since this is much easier than trying to wrestle them away from undesirable relationships later. It is worth making the effort to encourage your child to make friendships, which they can draw upon at home, and not just at school. Most children only spend two thirds of the year at school and even then, no more than 7 hours per day over 5 days. Having friends they can call on during these non-school times is essential. It is likely that most of these potential friends will also be school friends. More importantly, parents can be more actively involved in trying to shape relationships and getting to know the families of their child's friends. The parent's role is mainly to create *opportunities* for social contacts to take place rather than actually making friendships for their children. Opportunities can be very simple such as inviting a friend home to watch TV or play a computer game. Encouraging Interaction is the key, rather than attempting to organize sophisticated activities. With older children and adolescents, activities outside the home can be encouraged, particularly if other children share the same interests.

CHILD AND YOUTH CULTURE

As part of attending to the social environment as a way of promoting healthy psychological and behavioural development, parents need to take account of the wider cultural influences on young people. This is, of course, different from the culture adults are familiar with and it pays parents to take an interest in it, but not to the extent that this becomes intrusive for young people. There is nothing worse to a young person, than a parent who adopts the language, taste, style and other elements of youth culture.

This culture is difficult to define; it changes with time and changes with the age of young people. It is made up of many different things including music, language, entertainment, fashion, leisure activities, and ways that young people interact with each other. This type of culture has a valuable role in healthy child development. It helps young people develop a sense of identity that is different from adults. It also becomes a way of developing common interests with other young people and promotes relationship building. Most importantly, these cultural elements tend to meet some aspects of young peoples' developmental needs in a much more responsive way than the adult world can provide for. Part of its usefulness is its fast moving nature. This is best seen with technology where young people embrace rapid change very easily in a way that their parents often find difficult. Without a sub-culture that embraces such technological change, I would argue that technological change would be held up, or continue at a much slower pace. This of course, has not escaped the notice of manufacturers, who target young people when trying to market products. Young people lead, and the rest of us follow: they spend hours downloading music onto MP3 players and texting on sophisticated mobile phones, quickly embracing the next generation of electronic gadgetry

I remember my childhood in which I had enormous fun with simple board games, toys such as model cars and farm animals and simple storybooks. Now there are sophisticated electronic toys, games computers and a whole range of electronic gadgets and processes based on digital information technology, ranging from music to the cinema. Great! Child and youth culture not only reflects these changes but also helps young people take advantage of them.

I think parents need to develop an accepting and encouraging attitude to child and youth culture and yet at the same time, help young people to take advantage of it within acceptable boundaries. There might, for example, be a craze of collecting cards with one theme or another. Perhaps a new film or cartoon hits the cinema, starting a craze for all the memorabilia that goes with it. Parents will need to negotiate what are acceptable levels of interest and expenditure so that young people do not get overly obsessed to the exclusion of other things, or put unacceptable levels of financial pressure on parents.

I know of some parents who find all of this unacceptable and many have tried, as I see it, to "hold back the clock" and bring children up, essentially as they had been. I have known some parents to refuse to have TV at home and to discourage electronic toys. Some children bought up in certain religious communities are not allowed exposure to these things. The latter may be less of a problem if children, when they become adults, stay in these communities. For others, though, who have to make their way in the wider world, I do not think overly restricting their exposure to the wider child and youth culture will be helpful. I think it limits the healthy development of broad based social skills and prevents children from understanding the quality and speed of wider developments in society including social, technological, and cultural aspects.

SPIRITUAL, MORAL AND RELIGIOUS MATTERS

The spiritual and religious beliefs of parents can form an important aspect of parenting style and be of influence on the wider social world of the child. Families who have religious affiliations and who belong to social groups based on religious beliefs have, it seems to me, added advantages in their parenting approaches and styles. I will not discuss the merits or de-merits of particular religions or indeed, the value of religious faith at all. This would be far beyond the scope of the book. I am however, struck by the benefits of a set of values that stems from religious beliefs. The advantages here are that they have stood the test of time, they are (usually) well thought out and are promoted by a community, and at times, it has to be said, by nation states. This gives parents an authority and validation beyond the confines of the family home. It becomes so much easier, for example, to persuade young people of the value of a particular rule e.g. not abusing substances or having sex outside marriage, if this is not just a parental preference, but condemned by the wider community, as an aspect of day-to-day life, in regular teachings and set out in religious texts. Because of this, it seems to me that parents who have religious beliefs and are part of a functioning religious community, have some added advantages. It may not always seem like it to those parents. Many young people, particularly in adolescence, challenge these and other rules particularly when they conflict with other values, such as those held by peers or promoted in popular culture. Despite this, the research evidence suggests that young people can respect parental values even when they conflict with other values. In the long term, they are more likely to hold onto reasonable parental values. The process of challenging and questioning is a vital part of adolescent development and parents must not be too fazed by these conflict situations.

Even without religious beliefs, parents can promote valuable learning in young people by teaching them spiritual and moral values. This does not have to be as heavy a task, or as formal as it sounds, but whenever naturally occurring opportunities arise, it is well worth explaining the moral values that underpin a particular belief or attitude that you may have. Why it that you believe honesty is important? Why it is that stealing is wrong? By doing this, young people are helped to understand what issues underpin key elements of their parents' authority and style. More importantly, they can then predict parental reactions to new situations or incidents, which may not have occurred before. This avoids problems before they arise and reduces potential conflict situations.

Ah yes, you may say, but this assumes parents have all the answers and "have it all together" before they become parents. Far from it: I think that the process of bringing up children actually helps parents develop spiritual and moral qualities. In other words, it assists parental development as well. A similar situation exists with clinical trainees and myself. By having to explain what I do and teach others, it makes me examine my own practice and try to get it as right as I can. Without the stimulus of this process, I might be a poorer clinician. Children are good for adults!

BIOLOGICAL AND PHYSICAL ASPECTS

To a large extent, biological aspects are not easily changed and because of this, parents need to assist young people to either take advantage of particular skills and aptitudes or to cope with, and minimise any impairment. It is impossible to discuss all permutations, but the important thing here is to develop an appreciation of the biological influences on your child so that your parenting style and strategies are realistic and meet the needs of your child. For example, it would be foolish to strive to help your child become a top class athlete if he or she showed no inclination or aptitude for sport of any kind and was, for example, showing instead, an aptitude for music.

Physical Health Problems
Many children are born with, or acquire physical health problems. These can have a profound effect on their psychological well-being and personal development

Successful Parenting - The Four Step Approach

> *Jodie* developed epilepsy at 5 years of age. At first, it took the form of episodes in which she would lose concentration and forget what had gone on during these brief moments, which lasted 1-2 minutes. At 7 years of age, the epilepsy had worsened and developed into episodes involving shaking and twitching movements down her right side and occasional drop attacks when she would fall to the ground. Jodie had been started on anti-convulsant drug medication at 5 years of age and this medication had been changed regularly to try to control the worsening episodes. The illness had quite marked psychological affects on her. She hated the idea of taking tablets especially because there was no end in sight. She felt different from other children. She felt constantly vulnerable and not in charge of her own body. She became irritable, moody, and oppositional at home. Her parents were sympathetic and dealt with these issues effectively. Now, 10 years of age, Jodie still feels different, her self-esteem is low which seems to affect her ability to make friends and put the required effort into school related activities

In addition to medical problems such as Jodie's, many children are affected by developmental disorders such as delayed speech development or poor clarity of speech. Others may have poor motor coordination affecting gross motor skills such as running or hand-eye co-ordination. Fine motor skills may also be poor, resulting in children having poor handwriting skills. If severe enough, these types of problem might represent a dyspraxic disorder.

A common developmental problem is bedwetting with 15 out of every 100, five-year olds having frequent bedwetting episodes. Even at 10 years of age, 5 out of every 100 still have the problem. This, and other developmental disorders, can have quite marked psychological affects on young people. A problem such as bedwetting dramatically affects self-confidence, in that a child sees him or herself having a problem that they feel others of their age do not have and more significantly, it may seem to them, such a "babyish" problem. They may be wetting at night when their 3-year-old brother or sister is dry.

Learning Difficulties
Learning problems involving difficulties with memory, perceptual and literacy skills can also carry mental health risks. Other young people may have problems in concentrating and find it difficult to focus attention, maintain it for a reasonable length of time, or get easily distracted. All learning problems tend to undermine a child's self-esteem. Sometimes parents are taken by surprise at the extent and seriousness of psychological and behavioural problems that arise from learning difficulties.

Max was 17 years of age when his parents asked me to advise them on how to cope with him, particularly since his behaviour had worsened since leaving school. He was verbally aggressive, challenging, non-compliant and always negative. Max had developed epilepsy at 3 years of age and had been receiving treatment with anti-convulsant medication since that time. He was also dyslexic - probably related to the epilepsy. When he left school at 16 years of age, his reading age was at an 8-year level. It had long concerned his parents and teachers that he had low self-esteem. He constantly expressed unhappiness about his lack of accomplishments and abilities but refused to accept any praise for any of his successes. This was despite years of effort by the many adults in his life to encourage and support him. In many ways, I was not surprised by the presentation. Imagine what it was like for Max having an illness, which robbed you of control of your body and mind. How insecure he must have felt. Added to this, he had major difficulties in developing reading skills; something most of his friends had done with, as it seemed to him, little effort. Despite this, he had had considerable support and his behaviour had not been too problematic up to the time he had left school. He was now facing the adult world. He was not inclined to go to a college to further his education. He had a succession of manual jobs but he did not stick at these for any significant time .Most of these jobs however required some reading skills added to which, Max was not inclined to accept any form of authority. This I suspect was a product of his low

> *self-esteem. He often felt inferior to others and to counter this, to preserve as much self-esteem as he could, it was important for him never to concede this or put himself in a situation where he was constantly reminded of his reading difficulties.*
>
> *Max's troubled behaviour and particularly his aggression to his parents was the outcome of many years of frustration. This had now increasingly turned to anger. His parents were the only outlet for this. Who else, despite whatever he did or said, would stand by him? Even though his parents understood this, it did not help then to cope on a day-to-day basis. Max and his family were helped with family therapy. It has not resolved all the underlying difficulties, but Max is now more able to act less aggressively and impulsively and his parents are much more tolerant. In addition, all are working to help Max acquire a higher level of literacy skills and build up a belief in himself and his abilities.*

Physical characteristics

Children who are taller or smaller than the average can suffer from the unwanted attention of others and suffer psychologically. Most children who are significantly different from their friends and peers will attract a stigma that might also involve bullying and social rejection. The impact of small stature is probably easy for most of us to appreciate. Looking smaller than average can often result in others treating young people as if they are much younger than their chronological age. Many youngsters develop emotional problems because of this. Others often try to achieve a higher status by being assertive and appearing more socially mature for their age. In addition, parents may have a tendency to be overprotective and indulgent which may also have adverse effects on healthy psychological development.

Less well appreciated, is that young people who are taller than average for their age are also at risk of being emotionally handicapped. Tall children often feel overly conspicuous and as a consequence, embarrassed. Many have a tendency to try to play down their height by walking in a stooped manner and behaving in a less mature way, to counter the impression that they are older than they look. Many are surprised that tall children are vulnerable to bullying. This is however, not surprising. Tall children attract unwelcome attention for simply being too obviously different. Added to this, because they try to play down their size, including being overly passive, bullies succeed extremely well in victimising them.

It is worth noting that extremes of stature – tallness or smallness can be the result of medical disorders, nutritional factors or inherited familial traits. The important thing to be aware of is that it is easy to be unaware of the psychological effects of such biological factors, and parents need to be alert to the possible adverse effects on children. It is easy to overlook some of the problems associated with stature. Tallness, for example, for many adults is a desirable quality and they find it difficult to appreciate the occasional torment a tall youngster goes through because they feel "different". Remember, in early adolescence, being 'different' equals being 'odd'.

Birth Order and sibling relationships

It probably comes as no surprise to most parents that the psychological and behavioural development of children is in part, influenced by birth order. Before discussing birth order, do not feel too sorry for sole children. Research suggests that only children (without siblings), do not appear to grow up disadvantaged, socially or intellectually.

Most of us can appreciate that an older child may find it difficult to cope with the arrival of a new brother or sister. Many are likely to feel rejected and sidelined at the prospect of less parental, grandparental and other adult attention. This type of reaction will be much worse for those who have inherited temperamental difficulties to start with. The oldest children do, however, benefit from having close parental attention until the next child is born and some undoubtedly benefit by seeing themselves as the "senior" sibling. There is no hard and fast rule about these influences since much is an interaction between the personality of the eldest child and the influence of other biological as well as social and psychological factors. Parents, as I often say, must be watchful, monitor these things, and take them on board when making parenting decisions.

Subsequent children will often benefit from the improving skills and confidence of parents whose parenting experience is hopefully, getting better all the time. They may also benefit from the attention and care of older siblings in a way that older siblings do not. Younger children can get great satisfaction and learning value out of age appropriate play with older siblings. This will be invariably less satisfying and of less learning value to the older sibling but on the other hand, helps the development of healthy sibling relationships. It has been found that the oldest child tends to be academically stronger than subsequent children in the birth order, but that subsequent children are more emotionally stable.

Another issue of particular interest to developmental and child psychologists is the birth spacing between children. Research tells us that the ideal is same sex twins because both are at the same developmental stage, can occupy each other, with one having no particular psychological advantage over the other. In other words, one does not pose a particular threat to other. The next best scenario is children who are born more than three years apart. In this case, the age gap is so wide that they have their own interests and are not in competition with one another. They can also cooperate more easily, with the maturity of the older one being of additional help. For those of you with children approximately 3 years apart – yes, you've guessed it - you have the greatest likelihood of sibling conflict and rivalry. Such children are developmentally close and as a result, clashes occur. They compete for the same friends, space, toys, and parental attention. They are also more likely to be conscious of each other's abilities, with rivalry being a possible consequence. There is no easy solution to this, apart perhaps, from better family planning in future, but, there again; parents' find three-year gaps so convenient from a childcare and financial perspective, that it outweighs other considerations. The message here is that an understanding of these relationship dynamics needs to be integrated into the development of your parenting skills.

STEP 4
TECHNIQUES AND SRATEGIES

In this final part of the book, I want to give you coaching in a powerful set of strategies and techniques to assist your parenting. Psychologists, who were motivated to understand what determines, or shapes behaviour, whether in animals or humans, have developed these techniques, mainly during the 20th century. The extensive research was subsequently used to assist the development of techniques and therapies to assist people who had developed disturbed behaviour, mental health problems, and other types of behaviour, which caused them or others in society, problems. I will focus on a technique called Applied Behavioural Analysis which, coupled with techniques of Cognitive-Behaviour Modification, represents a powerful set of skills. Don't worry too much about the names of these approaches – it's more for background information. I will try to keep jargon to a minimum, given my basic belief that you don't need to be a psychologist to be a good parent. You will also find information on such techniques by other authors e.g. The Difficult Child by Stanley Turecki (1989) and there are also books for specific age groups, which you might find of value. Before we proceed, let's consider why we need such techniques.

THE SELF V OTHERS

You may wonder, after reading through Steps 1 to 3, why it is that we need special techniques and strategies. Surely, with all these things in place that we have discussed, young people and parents can get on in perfect harmony: parents will have clear expectations and young people will respond appropriately. Both you and I know that things aren't quite that simple and the same isn't even true of adult behaviour. We all know, for example, the law in respect of motoring. Despite this, people break speed limits, park illegally, drive without insurance etc. This is also a feature of other aspects of life where there are laws, rules, regulations, expectations, and moral obligations. An obvious question is why don't people simply conform to, or obey, these social requirements? For the most part, we all do, but just occasionally, we don't. The reason relates to struggle between the needs of the self and balancing those with the needs of others.

Take for example a Mum who is driving to school to pick up a child, but who is running late. She could get to the school and be 10 minutes late if she kept within the speed limits, but cut that to being 5 minutes late by breaking them. This is not of course a good enough reason for breaking speed limits. She decides to break them rather than keep her child waiting. We can all relate to this but might condemn it at the same time, given that we are all interested in improving road safety.

This type of "Self vs. Society" struggle is the major reason why we are unable to trust individuals to 'do what is right'. We have developed systems of penalties to enforce laws and regulations to ensure individuals and groups comply with such rules. More subtly, even where no laws exist for certain issues, moral obligations and the unwritten rules governing social relationships (e.g. manners, courtesy, protocol etc) work to get people to comply through various emotional states such as satisfaction, pleasure, guilt or rejection. If people don't comply, they are made to feel uncomfortable – if they do, they may be shown appreciation. These emotional consequences tend to keep people 'on track'.

Sometimes people behave in a way which does not particularly affect others but is only harmful to themselves. A child who becomes socially withdrawn, overly negative, inattentive in a classroom, or who eats too much is not likely to alienate others, but is at risk of personal, developmental or mental health difficulties. Parents frequently need to get involved to change behaviour in these types of circumstances and the strategies suggested here are every bit as useful.

> *Sound Parenting involves appreciating that conflicts between our own needs and those of others are a normal part of life for all of us, including children and that few, if any of us, always stick to the rules and comply with expectations all the time. It is tougher for young people because they are still in the process of learning about these issues and the benefits or penalties associated with compliance or non-compliance.*

WHAT IS BEHAVIOUR?

Throughout this section on techniques and strategies I will, for simplicity, talk about changing *behaviour*. I apologise for this because it seems such a cold, restrictive term. Unfortunately, there is not a good substitute word in the English language. The term behaviour is very much psychological shorthand for many types of action or response. This includes actual motor behaviour such as leg, arm, facial and hand movements as well as more complex acts such as hitting, biting, self-harm and so on. Most importantly, it also can describe other actions and responses, which we think of as emotions. These too can, of course, be simple as well as complex. Sometimes we can only guess at their presence through actions. For example, acts of physical or verbal aggression might indicate the presence of anger. Emotional negativity might be indicated by a child frequently complaining that nothing ever works out right for them or that other people are always being mean to them. The term 'behaviour' might also describe verbal actions such as talking and shouting. It might refer to more subtle communications including body language. It can also include concepts such as 'attitude', 'motivation' 'attention' etc. In other words, I will use the word behaviour to refer to virtually the whole range of human actions and activities. We are interested in them here, because many are undesirable and you as a parent will want to help your child to change or modify them. For these, I will often use the phrase 'target behaviours'.

DESCRIBING TARGET BEHAVIOURS AND EMOTIONS

A key first task is to learn how to see clearly the behaviour, or set of behaviours, that you want to change. This might sound strange as it may well be immediately obvious to you what behaviours need to be changed. The problem is that everyday descriptions of behaviour used by all of us are often very general and inadequate in helping us bring about change. Here are three everyday examples.

- She's attention seeking.
- He's always naughty.
- He never does what I ask him to do.

These descriptions are good enough for conversational purposes but not to understand fully what it is you want to change and what it is you want your child to attend to. 'Attention seeking', if we were to describe it more accurately, might for example, mean that the young person is

a) constantly verbally interrupting a parent when they are speaking on the 'phone
b) verbally and physically interrupting when friends or visitors enter the house
c) unable to occupy themselves in play without constantly wanting parental involvement

These specific descriptors are the basis of starting to encourage changes in behaviour. They provide a basis for talking clearly with young people about the issues you want to address and are helpful in avoiding disputes between you and your child about whether a particular behaviour has changed or not. A common example of this is the parent who attempts to change behaviour but defines desirable change as 'being a good boy for the day'. Now what young James sees as his being good all day might be a whole lot different from what his parent expects! For him, an improvement might, for example, involve hitting his younger sister just once during the day as opposed to several times a day.

ANALYSING BEHAVIOUR – KNOWING YOUR ABC

In this section, I want to encourage you to see problem behaviour in a different way from that which you are probably used to. This is the key to bringing about change. The essence of the approach is to break problem behaviour down into three key parts. Understanding the importance to behaviour of these three parts is the basis of developing skills in *changing* behaviour. After a while, it is surprising how looking at behaviour in this new way becomes second nature.

Happily, given that it is a key learning task, the three parts have the acronym **ABC** that stands for:-

ANTECEDENTS- events that occur *before* the behaviour

BACKGROUND - in which the behaviour occurs

> **THE BEHAVIOUR ITSELF**

CONSEQUENCES-the events which occur *after* the behaviour

Encouraging any change in behaviour may involve altering one or all of these elements, since any one, or all of them, will influence when and how, the behaviour occurs and the nature of that behaviour.

Antecedents are events that, through observation, you notice happen *just before* a target behaviour i.e. the one you want to change, occurs. The events can be physical behaviour (by the child or others) or talk, smells, visual, noises etc. Any of these may last from seconds to many minutes. An important thing to remember is that you must try hard not to make a judgement about what events are relevant or irrelevant to the target behaviour before you have observed, listed, and evaluated them. The way to narrow down the key antecedent event or events is to consider all of the instances of when the target behaviour occurred and try to identify any type of event that consistently appeared to trigger the target behaviour. Even then, there might be several. In this case, you can do one, two, or all of three things.

1. The most common method is to use your judgement, to check through several sets of observations looking for events that seem relevant. Equally, use your intuition to pick out ones that seem likely to be implicated in, contributing to, or causing the target behaviour.

2. Do a little experiment if possible, where you engineer things to exclude some antecedent events as outlined above but keeping other ones in place. If all goes well you can narrow down the field so that you can identify the key event.

3. For most children and young people, just ask them! Find a calm moment in the day, when they are reasonably happy and receptive and talk through with them their view of what happens typically before a target event occurs. This can include thoughts, feelings and actual behaviours either by themselves or with others.

Background refers to aspects of the emotional, physical, and social world of the child that may be of significance in bringing the target behaviour about or affecting its severity. We covered many of these in **STEP 3**. The following illustrate the range of possibilities:

- Your child may be having difficulties with peers
- You may be swamped with problems of your own that reduce your ability or willingness to play, talk or just *be* with your child
- Your child has a full day at school, comes home, and is bored/tired/hungry/excited/depressed/unhappy because of events at school or on the way home.
- The pressure of homework may be causing stress and irritability.
- There may be exceptional health, developmental or other biological influences at work.

Find out what the relevant background factors are by using strategies 1 and 3 set out above to identify antecedents. In addition, it might also be helpful to get the views of other people, particularly family and friends who know your family well and whom you can trust, to come up with sensible ideas. For relevant school based background factors, your child's class teacher or form tutor may, in a similar way, be able to help.

One very important thing worth remembering is that young people (and all of us for that matter) can become stressed by not just one event, but a succession of minor ones. These events do not have to be big or serious ones, in fact, they might be described by the young person as being neutral or even pleasurable. Added together though, they can become a significant source of stress. A common example of this is a change of school. There is a new environment to cope with, new friends, a loss of old friends, new teachers, different routine etc. Your child may report that things are "OK" and even enjoyable, but these changes will be taking their toll on their physical and mental stamina. They may not represent obvious problems as such, but may lie at the heart of other problems. You child's simple act of non-compliance at home over a trivial request can conceivably be caused or exacerbated by the stress of coping at school, even though your child says things are fine there.

Consequences refer to an event or events, which develop after the target behaviour has occurred. This may include behaviour, talk, social disruption, feelings, attitudes and anything else you can think of. The key thing is to spot events that arise after the target behaviour, which wouldn't have arisen had it not have been for the behaviour itself.

Enough theory! Let me give some examples of the ABC method of analysis and change. Remember, this is a way of looking at not only problem behaviour but also everyday behaviour. Changing the behaviour can be bought about by changing the antecedents, the background, the consequences or any combination of these. There are many examples from motoring, to which I hope you can relate. I have chosen these because hopefully, both men and women can relate to them. Let me now take you through some examples.

Changing antecedent events
A friend of mine had great difficulty in parking his cars in a rather cramped garage. Either the car would be too far forward,

making it difficult to walk around it, or too far back, in which case the garage door would not shut. Rarely could he park it in the correct position. There was no **Background** issue of any relevance nor was any **Consequence** event important. The problem was with the **Antecedent** events. The critical factor was either my friends inability to *use* visual cues to help with the parking or the *lack* of such cues in the garage. The solution was a simple one. He suspended a tennis ball from the ceiling in such a way that it touched the front windscreen only when the car was in the correct position. My friend did not analyse the problem in this way. He, as well as you and I might, was able to work it out by using his intuition. For many problems though, this does not work and this is where a more analytical approach comes in useful.

Changing Background events
Many rural villages near where I live have experienced road traffic accidents and in many cases, measures to improve road safety have been implemented, most notably, traffic calming measures (road humps). This is obviously an effort to change antecedent events i.e. excessive speed. However, attempts were also made to change background events simply by placing signs at each village boundary saying, "Please drive carefully through our village". Hopefully this now raises driver awareness of safety issues.

Changing consequences
A common, undesirable motoring behaviour is breaking speed limits which traffic authorities would, in the interests of road safety, like to change. In addition to changing background

and antecedent events, changing consequences has become one of the main stays of policy. The problem is, that drivers are often 'rewarded' for breaking the speed limit by getting to where ever they want to go more quickly. An obvious solution is to alter the likely consequence for speeding drivers so that they are deterred instead of encouraged by their behaviour. Speed/Safety cameras, speed displays at the roadside and police speed checks all make it possible to apprehend drivers and allow fines (punishments) to be imposed. Changing the consequence in this way is likely to reduce the probability of speed violations in the future

Changing all three aspects

Finally lets consider how we might change all 3 elements using the example of eating one sandwich too many!

A SANDWICH?

A *I see a pack of sandwiches for sale in a shop or filling station between meals*

B *my appetite has been stimulated by biological processes*

BEHAVIOUR | *I purchase the sandwiches.*

C *my hunger goes and (hopefully) I feel good.*

*This is an everyday occurrence and would not be a problem unless I was overweight (I'm not - at least, at the time of writing!) and was trying to control my food consumption. If this was the case, my tendency to purchase sandwiches between meals could be target behaviour for change. In this case, I could usefully make some changes to all three elements of the **ABC**. I can influence the power of the **antecedent event** by avoiding temptation by staying clear of shops with sandwiches by taking a different route from my usual one. I can reduce the power of the **background** event (hunger) by drinking fluid (a fizzy drink perhaps) instead or eating a low calorie food such as a piece of fruit. Finally, I could alter the **consequences,** by making sure that instead of feeling good, I felt bad. I could for example, keep a picture of a fat me in my pocket to remind me of what I am trying to change. After eating, the sight of it may make me feel a little less content.*

Now let us look at more relevant examples using the Richards and Moss families as examples The Richards' daughter Emma was presenting with a fairly straightforward problem which is a simple way to illustrate the ABC principles. Carl Moss and his family were struggling with a more complex set of problems but this I find to be more reflective of the type of situation that drives parents to despair.

> **Mrs Richards** *had a problem most mornings getting her 9-year-old daughter Emma to school. She also had to take her younger daughter, Kate to nursery afterwards and often the delays caused Kate to be late, making the situation even worse. An ABC analysis did not reveal any key **background** event. Emma went to bed in good time and was not overly tired in the mornings. She also enjoyed school, which Emma agreed on, as did her class teacher. It was unlikely that any **consequence** was an important maintaining factor. Mrs Richard's tended to give Emma a hard time with verbal disapproval, which lasted from the time they left home to the time they got to school. Clearly, it was having no, or a minimal, effect. There was an **antecedent** event of possible importance in that Emma had a TV in her room and tended to watch TV as she was getting dressed. Mrs Richards discussed the issues with Emma and they both agreed that that the TV was a problem. This example illustrates that Mrs Richards had carefully considered all aspects of the ABC one by one and was content that she had identified the factor that was the issue with Emma and they both agreed that that the TV contributing to the problem.*

*She worked out with Emma what desirable behaviour she wanted instead and came up with a technique for bringing about change. Mrs Richards used one of the punishment strategies detailed later on in **Step 4**, which involved using the withdrawal of a privilege as a punishment. She told Emma that she would not be allowed to watch TV the next morning if she did not come out of her bedroom, ready for school by 8.00 am on any given morning. Mrs Richards was not too sure this would work and had it in mind to stop Emma watching TV when she came home from school, when her favourite program was on. She did say to Emma that she might well do this if Emma did not respond to the first plan. As it happened, Emma responded well and over the first 3 weeks, only lost her morning TV viewing on three mornings. Each time the privilege was withdrawn Emma made sure she was ready for school the next day.*

Successful Parenting - The Four Step Approach

Mrs Moss *dreaded the times when her 10-year-old son Carl returned home from school. This for her was quite often at the end of a busy day. Since her younger child, Amy, had been born, 5 years ago, she had gradually built up a return to paid employment and had tried to fit this around childcare commitments. She tended to pick Amy up from School at 3.00 pm, go home, and be there for Carl, who walked home himself and usually arrived at 3.45 pm. By this time, she was tired and just wanted to put her feet up. Instead, she had to give Amy some time to talk about her day and give her something to eat, by which time, Carl tended to arrive home.*

Carl had attended his current school since he was 5 years of age. He generally had got on well socially as well as making good progress academically. Of late, he had been experiencing difficulty with friendships. His good friend, whom he had known since the first year, had left the school and the neighbourhood at the beginning of the previous term and although Carl had other friends, none was as close. At lunchtimes and some break-times, he was left out of football games, which he tended not to be too interested in anyway.

Carl often came home from school and displayed a range of disruptive behaviours and attitudes towards his Mum and sister, Amy. On returning from school, he would enter the home, dropping his coat and rucksack on the hall floor. This then usually resulted in Mrs Moss asking Carl to pick up his coat and take his rucksack to his room, which he usually refused to do. The same happened when she asked him to change his clothes. On most days, Mrs Moss finished up shouting at Carl and issuing threats such as depriving him of television or withdrawing pocket money. Quite often, these 'punishments' were not carried out, partially carried out, or left until Mr Moss came home in the evening. More often than not, things had settled down by then and the incidents forgotten about. After the initial battle between Carl and his mother, Carl would usually eat a light snack that his Mum would prepare. He then tended to settle down to watch TV but this often resulted in argumentative behaviour between Carl and Amy. Most often, this would arise from Carl insisting on watching programmes of his choice but refusing to allow his sister her choice. On many occasions, this degenerated into Carl being physically aggressive towards Amy. Mrs Moss than tended to intervene, often sending Carl to his room. After this period of "Time Out", Carl would return downstairs but for two or three more hours, his behaviour would be confrontational and argumentative, particularly if his Mum tried to encourage him to do any homework that he was supposed to do. The situation only became less fraught when Dad returned home at 7.00 pm. Carl tended to respond well to his father's presence and the evening would tend to end calmly with Carl enjoying spending time with the other family members before going to bed.

Now let us analyse this in terms of the **ABC** and see how the Moss's worked through the problem. Richard and Judy Moss, the parents, decided that there should be two target behaviours for change;-

1. Carl's actions on first entering the house i.e. throwing his coat and rucksack on the hall floor and failing to change out of his school clothes.

2. Although the aggressive behaviour to Amy was perhaps the more important target, it was felt that if Carl complied with his mother's wishes on arrival at home, the improvement in emotional climate between Carl and his mother would probably reduce the likelihood of aggression towards Amy. Even so, a plan was implemented to reduce the frequency of his annoying behaviour towards his sister as well.

Antecedents

After much thought, Judy Moss came to understand that as Carl came home, the act of his throwing down his clothes and school bag immediately upset her. Mrs Moss was generally a tidy person and was keen for Carl to change out of his school uniform as soon as he returned from school. The fact that he did neither, tended to make her angry within minutes of Carl crossing the doorstep. As a result, she realised that her body language, facial expressions, and voice were likely to be giving out rather negative vibes to Carl and probably made him more likely to be oppositional.

Background

A wider analysis of the whole situation that Richard Moss spotted is that both Judy and Carl were ill prepared emotionally, for any conflict every school day afternoon. Carl and his mother were often, more likely that not, to be tired, upset, stressed or just unhappy before either arrived home on a given day. This made both vulnerable to irritability, impulsive and unfriendly behaviour. Mrs Moss also felt alone in having to deal with Carl for several hours before her husband came home, which in turn, increased her stress levels and sense of helplessness. If that wasn't bad enough, both Carl and his mother had had very little to eat since lunchtime adding to their tendencies to be irritable. A further issue, which Judy and Richard identified, was the presence of sibling rivalry between Carl and Amy. He seemed to have had some difficulty in accepting that Amy had a right to her mother's time and attention.

Consequences
Carl's action in the hallway seemed to set off a chain reaction. His mother's negative reactions seemed more likely than not to make him sullen and irritable which may have explained his tendency to selfish and aggressive behaviour towards his sister. Another important element is that Carl's behaviour, within minutes of his arriving home, resulted in sharp verbal exchanges between Carl and his mother. Psychologists have long recognised that children value parental attention. Less well understood by many parents is that this, from a parents' point of view, doesn't have to be 'good attention'. This is particularly true if, for one reason or another, a child is not able to experience a sufficient amount of calm, loving attention from a parent. A child who, for example, acts in an oppositional and defiant way, rapidly gets parental attention. Few other kinds of behaviour so reliably achieve this. It is also true, that this type of parental attention can be extended indefinitely – just try

temper tantrums, throwing objects, bashing your sibling etc. Because the Moss's had invested sufficient time to analyse the problems, they had enough information to work out a strategy to put things right. The Moss's looked at all three elements i.e. antecedent events, background events and consequences. They used some of the techniques detailed later in this section to modify antecedent and consequential events with considerable success. You can also probably guess the changes that were made to alter the background events that were adding considerably to the problems.

PRIORITISING PROBLEMS

As the Moss's situation illustrates, there may be more than one undesirable behaviour that you feel needs attention. **Don't be tempted to try to change everything at once.** It's too much to take on, is less likely to work and is not necessary anyway. The key to success is to **pick on no more than two or three target behaviours** and focus on those. The tricky part is which ones to go for. Here are three tips.

1. Don't choose the most difficult problem. This will be the type which has been the most difficult, longstanding, and resistant to previous efforts to bring about change. It is also likely to be one that your child has shown little inclination to change. Instead, choose a target behaviour that your child is able to produce sometimes but not all the time. In other words, a desirable behaviour, which your child produces occasionally, but not reliably or consistently.

2. Choose a target behaviour which you feel is likely to be achieved. This may be because your child can be signed up to making the change, because they produce it most of the time anyway, or you feel you have a good strategy of reinforcement or punishment that is likely to work.

3. One of the great things about working to achieve a desirable change in behaviour is that success breeds success. If you can work with your child to achieve change in one area, it has a knock on effect in another. Most often, this is because one successful change gives parents and young people such encouragement that the gains from making other needed changes look more desirable. These other desired changes often just occur without a special programme. Your child simply sees the value in complying and feels good about the achievement. This is why choosing a target that is likely to be achieved is important, given the beneficial knock on effects on other targets.

RECORDING AND MEASURING

Throughout this section, I will be encouraging you to use specific techniques but only use them if they work. You will only know if they work if you keep a record of some kind. Before implementing any strategy, find out first how often the problem behaviour happens. This can be part of the observational techniques and part of the ABC approach that I will be describing later. The recording needn't be anything too complicated – just a simple count of how often the behaviour occurs each hour, day, or week depending on how often it generally happens. There is no point in recording hourly, something that happens two or three times per week. You can do a simple tally count i.e. recording each occurrence of the behaviour, if the target behaviours are not happening that often. If they are happening very frequently, then a global rating is better. For this, just make a rating at the end of a period such as a day, of how bad you think the problem was - ten if it's the worst you have ever known it to be, ranging down to zero if it didn't happen at all.

When you implement your strategy to change a given behaviour, try to keep a similar record of how you are getting on. For some of the programmes, you may be keeping some form of record anyway, in the form of a Token System, Star Chart, diary etc. explained in further detail later in this chapter. For others, keeping a log of progress is essential. I have found that it is not usually a good enough guide for parents to rely on their overall view of how well any change programme is progressing. This is particularly true of frequently occurring behaviours when it's vital to know if you are making any impact with a given programme. If Sam is pushing or shoving his little sister around 100 times per day, a reduction to 90 times or 80 times over successive days is worth knowing about even though you are a long way from resolving the problem. At least you will know if you are on the right track.

A further advantage of recording is that it can directly help to achieve whatever target you have set. By sharing your recorded observations with your child, this can be a powerful incentive for your child to change. It might be the first time that they have been made aware of just how many times they have done such and such. Still more powerful, the record sheets can be shown to other significant carers whom the child respects.

SPECIFIC TECHNIQUES

I have written at some length describing the ABC of change. What now follows is a description and tips on using a number of techniques. I have concentrated on ones that are generally useful in a very wide variety of situations and for many types of problems. In particular, these are helpful in bringing about change when you have identified either antecedent, consequential events or both as being important in causing and/or maintaining any target problem behaviour or behaviours. You will already be familiar with some but I would urge you nevertheless, to study the sections carefully. The reason for this is that I find that many of the techniques have become half understood. Many were developed from the work of behavioural psychologists, were then incorporated into easily understood techniques and have passed from one professional group to another and finally, onto parents. Frequently, key elements have been forgotten which then reduces the power of the techniques.

Reinforcement

The use of what psychologists call reinforcement is probably one of the chief methods of changing behaviour. Strictly defined, it is something that will increase the probability of a particular behaviour, thought or emotion occurring. The 'something' can be 'anything' in fact - money, a taste, smell, an experience, a toy, a hug etc. It can be anything that is encouraging or, to use psychological jargon, 'reinforcing'. There are many everyday examples of this with a few set out below. In these examples, the parts that serve as reinforcers are underlined.

- <u>Wages and salaries</u> increase the likelihood that employees will not only work, but the addition of bonuses, perks and other incentives will more likely than not, improve their commitment and the quality of their work.
- The act of gambling, such as putting money repeatedly into a fruit machine, is made more likely because of the occasional <u>payout or prize</u>.
- Emotional ties between people can be strengthened through mutual <u>praise and approval</u>.

- Applying perfumes and after-shave fragrances which produce a <u>pleasant smell</u>, may increase the attractiveness of the person using it.
- An artist, in producing a <u>visually appealing</u> painting, will increase the probability, that people will look at and purchase their work.

I often mention these everyday examples as a way of demonstrating to parents that we are all under the influence of reinforcers on a daily basis. I also use such everyday examples to counter the reluctance of some parents to use reinforcement techniques because they regard it as using "bribery". To me, bribery smacks of an illicit, morally bad act, which reinforcement is not. Bribery is certainly a type of reinforcement, but most things, which serve as reinforcers, are not bribes.

A common misconception is that reinforcers have to be expensive items. Parental approval is probably the most commonly used and effective technique available to parents that is usually greatly reinforcing. It is a mistake to think that you always have to use money, sweets, gifts etc. There may be a place for those, but the general idea is to use the cheapest, readily available thing that will encourage the probability of the desired thought, emotion, or behaviours taking place.

I strongly advocate reinforcement techniques because they are based on encouragement. This is particularly important if your child is experiencing feelings of low self worth. Feelings of low self-worth or esteem often develop in tandem with emotional and behavioural problems. When a child has a poor opinion of him or herself, bad or inappropriate behaviour may not trouble them too much. After all, others see them as being troublesome (to say the least), they see themselves in the same way so if they are criticised or punished, so what – they can't feel any worse and it's further confirmation of how worthless they feel. By using positive techniques to bring about change, young people with low self-esteem are more likely to comply and a further benefit is that it will help bring an improvement in their feelings of self-worth. There are further benefits to parents of positive techniques. Giving punishments is tiring, unsatisfying, and often confrontational. Many parents spend a disproportionate amount of time punishing their children – most often verbally but also withdrawing privileges, smacking etc to the extent that parenting becomes a chore, a pain and depressing. Such parents end up being the type of parent they never wanted to be. It is far more satisfying to use positive parenting techniques based on encouragement and reward rather than on punishment. Most importantly, using positive techniques help to re-build any parent-child relationship that may have suffered over weeks, perhaps months of clashes.

How do I spot a reinforcer?

There is no one thing that will work for all children in all circumstances. Always remember that a reinforcer is something that will increase the chance of a desired (target) response occurring. When children are old enough to talk in sentences, the best way to find an appropriate reinforcer is to discuss with them what they would find encouraging - within reason that is! They after all are in the best position to know what will motivate them. I never ceased to be pleasantly surprised how reasonable young people can be in doing this exercise. Rarely do they ask for outrageously expensive items or treats. In fact, their suggestions are often surprisingly reasonable and modest. For younger children, praise, hugs, clapping etc can all be hugely effective. Older ones may respond to Star Charts or other similar systems in which, for example they can earn points, which can be exchanged for a variety of things such a toys, money, trips out and other treats. I will focus now on describing two main types of reinforcement approaches: praise and encouragement and token systems.

Praise and Encouragement
These are probably the most natural, easiest, and effective forms of reinforcement. The reason they are so effective, is that they tap a basic biological need in most of us for social approval. They are even more powerful when they originate from people we respect, or with whom we have close emotional ties. For children, parents, siblings, extended family members and teachers all have a massive potential to influence.

Most parents use praise and encouragement perfectly naturally. In fact, our children's responses are generally reinforcing for us, which in turn increases the probability that we will use them repeatedly. In this section however, I want to encourage you to use praise and encouragement more thoughtfully and specifically. Hopefully, they will naturally occur to you as a possible strategy after doing your **ABC** in respect of a given problem. There are a few basic rules to follow:

- **Be clear** over what it is you want to praise or encourage. Don't expect your child to "be a good boy or girl" over the course of a day. Be clear in your own mind what *specific* behaviour it is you want to encourage and let your child know what it is you want to praise.

- **Be specific** about what desired response you want to encourage. This means avoiding global praise such as "good girl" or "you have been brilliant today". Much better would be "Well done for tidying your room today as you promised" or "You have been really great in getting yourself ready for school by 8.00 am today"

- **Be prompt** in giving praise and encouragement. Praise and encouragement, like other types of reinforcement, work very much better when delivered immediately after the desired behaviour has occurred. Sometimes this is not practicable but as long as the delay is reasonable from your child's point of view, the technique will be effective.

- **Be consistent** by acknowledging and praising all occurrences of the desired behaviour. Again this is not always possible but generally be on the look out for the behaviour you want to encourage. The need for such vigilance is one reason why it is best not to choose more than two or three target behaviours for any programme of change.

- **Be effective** by using *appropriate* praise and encouragement. Like other types of reinforcement, there are none that will suit all children in all circumstances. You know your child best and you should be able to gauge what types of praise and encouragement are effective for your child. Some young people are OK with gushing over-the-top deliveries of verbal praise whilst others will secretly wish that the ground would open up and swallow them. Remember that in giving praise: deliver it purposefully, directly in front of your child and not for example, in the form of an off-hand remark from the next room.

A child who doesn't like praise?

A common problem parents find in using praise and encouragement is that some children seem averse to praise. "He hates being praised". This is common in young people who have, in psychological jargon, low self-esteem. They believe themselves to be inferior in a number of ways. In practical terms this means for example, not being able to make friends, not being 'good' at sport, reading, writing, making things etc. The young person often has become so used to running himself or herself down, seeing him or herself as incompetent, that *any* praise is taken to be false. I have heard many young people say, "They don't really mean it" or "I get embarrassed" when they receive praise. If this sounds like your child, it is important that you accept this and not "force" praise on a child. After all, if it's aversive to your child, it's not a reinforcer. It will in fact, act instead like a punishment and reduce the probability of the desired behaviour taking place.

The first thing to attend to is to check that you are using the most appropriate type of praise and encouragement. Young people who have low self-esteem tend to be older children and adolescents. Their stage of development enables you to talk to them and gently explore what they feel is for them, comfortable praise and encouragement. Quite often, I find that they simply want low-key praise and recognition or they want it in private and not in front of brothers and sisters, for example.

The second approach is, in addition to reworking your praise delivery, to focus more on the token systems outlined below. These deliver appropriate reinforcement but verbal reinforcement need only be a minimal component.

Token Systems
Token systemsThe essence of token schemes is that in return for achieving a given target, the young person earns some sort of a 'token' that can signify, or be traded for, a reward. These tokens can be stars, stickers (such as smiley faces), points, or some pictorial representation such as a drawing of the sought reward. The great benefit is convenience, in that you do not have to have the actual reward to hand during the time when it is being earned. This becomes particularly useful when the rewards are intangible such as watching a special TV programme, going to the cinema etc. Another great advantage is that the tokens can be rewarding in themselves. The best example is a star chart, in that for some very young children, there is no need to make it so that the stars can be

traded for something else; they value the stars in their own right. An example from the adult world, of an effective token system, is money. It is useless in its own right. You cannot do much with a piece of paper or bit of metal. In the past, a bank note could be exchanged at the Bank of England for its equivalent value in gold. This is what gave the bank note its value. Even though, regrettably, this is no longer possible, the system works because we all have confidence in the token value of notes and coins.

Star Charts

Most parents are probably familiar with giving children stars on a chart if only because it and its variants are commonly used in Primary Schools to recognise learning achievements, effort, and appropriate behaviour. Choose three or four target behaviours you want to encourage and each time they occur, place a star on the chart. Instead of stars, stickers such as 'smiley faces' or ones with words such as "Well Done" can be used. These are usually available from stationers. Equally, you can devise a chart where your child can colour in various shapes as an alternative. As I will emphasis later with token systems, it is important to reinvent them every now and then to keep your child's interest, so try several different styles. Star Charts can be made more potent by offering rewards when your child earns a given target number of stars/stickers etc. This helps to extend the usefulness of these charts to children in middle childhood.

Point Systems

1. Star Chart Systems are very useful for young children but they may not appeal to older children. A points system is more flexible, works for longer, and is suitable for older children and younger teenagers. The idea is that targets, and usually I suggest no more than three or four at the most, should be agreed with your child, after your ABC analysis has identified the most appropriate targets to aim for.

2. The next step is to agree how many points achieving a certain target will earn. The number really does not matter. The main thing to work on is the difference in values between the different targets. You are likely to want to reward the more difficult and demanding tasks at a higher level than some easier ones.

3. Next, agree with your child what the points can be used for. The best way forward, is to think of as many things as you can, putting a price on each. This can be favourite toys, money, watching special videos or DVDs, going on a special trip, having a story read etc. Try to choose a range of things of different values since this will ensure that your child's interest will be maintained. As a minimum, there should be something that they can exchange the points for after a couple of days of achieving the targets reasonably well. You therefore need to make a reasonable estimate of what they can realistically achieve each day to make the exercise encouraging for them. If it is too difficult, they will lose interest. The great thing about this system is that you can agree on easily earned items as well as

more costly ones, which may take your child several days, or weeks to earn. This is particularly appropriate for older children who will have the patience and incentive to see this through.

4. Use a chart to plot your child's progress. This should detail the targets, the days of the week and the points earned. An important thing to remember is to complete the chart as soon as possible after the target behaviour has occurred. This in itself, for most children will be reinforcing. They will not necessarily be able to spend the points at the time but the act of earning them is, in itself, satisfying. Added to this, use verbal praise, hugs, or other naturally favourable responses that you know your child will appreciate. The progress chart can help inform other family members who are not present at the time but who can see it later and, again, give even more praise if, this is judged to be reinforcing.

5. Once your child has earned a reward through acquiring sufficient points, try to give it as soon as possible, within reason. If the points are to be exchanged for money, this is best done as soon as possible, if not immediately. If it is for a trip the cinema for, example, there can be a longer delay because your child will not think it unreasonable to have to wait a few hours or a couple of days.

6. After a few weeks, think about adding more rewards to maintain your child's interest in the scheme. If there are targets that are proving hard for your child to achieve, irrespective of the rewards on offer, you could increase

the points earned or add bonus points to make the scheme more attractive.

7. Point schemes have a limited shelf life. I often hear parents say, "I tried a Star Chart - it worked well for a while and then he/she lost interest". Great! It worked and yes, it doesn't work forever. This is of course, to be expected. Most of us tire or get bored with things after a while. Besides this, many schemes ask a lot of young people. There may be rewards on offer but they have to work hard in the face of old habits to earn them. The thing to do is to have a break from the scheme after two or three months. This should last as long as possible and then reinstate it. Incorporate new targets when old ones have been achieved and try to re-format the chart and offer different rewards. Better still perhaps, use another related system as described on page 130.

8. These schemes can be a focus of resentment or jealousy by other children in the family. To counter this, my usual advice is to include other children in the family, in the same or similar schemes. It is unlikely that you will not be able to think of targets for change in your other children and the flexibility of the points system means that it should be suitable for all but the youngest and oldest children.

<u>A note of caution.</u> It is possible to devise token schemes where you deduct points, stars etc. I would generally advise against doing this. Unless carefully designed, this can have a de-moralizing effect and threaten the whole scheme.

Kirsty *had gone through a troubled time with one crisis after another. Her parents' separated 3 years ago when she was 12 years old. Her Gran, with whom she was very close, died in the previous year and she was feeling stressed by revision work for exams over the past few months. Her Mum had found a new partner who 12 months ago, moved in with them with his two children. Given that Kirsty had two siblings as well, the house felt over crowded at times. Mrs Warren, Kirsty's Mum, had become concerned that Kirsty was becoming less willing to help with household chores, do homework and was starting to stay out with friends much too late at nights. Mrs Warren recognised that Kirsty was feeling somewhat pushed aside at home and resolved to spend more time with her on her own. She also wanted to avoid frequent arguments between them over these and other problems.*

She sat down with Kirsty and agreed three targets that did not represent either all of the difficulties or the worst of them. They were however, reasonably achievable and they both worked out the record system shown next. In discussing what the points could be traded for, Kirsty opted for money at an exchange rate of 5p for every point. The maximum she could earn, assuming that there was homework to do every night of the week, that the weather was fine enough every day to take the dog for a walk and she was well enough to go to the youth club each week, was £4.20. Mrs Warren felt that this was affordable added to the £5 per week that she would give Kirsty anyway.

Successful Parenting - The Four Step Approach

TARGET	MONDAY	TUESDAY	WEDNES-DAY	THURS-DAY	FRIDAY	SATUR-DAY	SUNDAY
1. Taking Rover for a walk							
2. Doing homework by 8.30 PM							
3. Being home by 11.00 PM on Thursdays							

1. 4 points to be earned for taking Rover for a walk lasting 15 minutes before dinner unless its raining, when 5 minutes will be OK.
2. 5 points to be earned for doing homework by 8.30 PM on the nights that it is set.
3. 3 points for being home by 10.30 PM on Thursdays after the Club finishes.

Pictorial schemes

These are useful because they add variety and interest to token systems and as such, are particularly suited to early childhood (three to five years of age). One variety sets out the main reward as a picture. Thus, if you have agreed that in return for a particular behaviour (or whatever the target is), your child can earn a football, you draw a picture of a football and divide it into sections, each of which can be earned each day. Happily, footballs are sectional items anyway, and so lend themselves well to this scheme.

An illustration of using this method is that chosen by George.

***George** was seven years of age when he started to become tardy in getting ready for school. There was no particular antecedent or background event of any significance, George just seemed to like to take his time, often breaking off from getting dressed to do other things. This had been getting worse and making his Mum frequently anxious about getting George to school on time. George's Mum and Dad decided that something had to be done and devised the scheme, illustrated next, which involved altering consequences. They felt that George was quite happy to take his time because there was no particular reason for him to hurry. They decided to develop a scheme to reward George for getting dressed by a target time each morning. George became enthusiastic about the idea of a reward scheme and was the one who came up with the idea of a football as a reward. He managed to complete all sections within two school weeks and on the last weekend, got his*

> *football. Thereafter, there was no problem in his getting ready for school. He seemed to have got into the habit of dressing without distraction. His Mum was much calmer which in itself was more pleasurable for George.*

George's Football Reward

Every time George gets himself dressed and ready for school by 8.00AM each day, he can colour in a section of the footballer. When 8 sections have been coloured in, we will buy a football.

Signed. Mum and Dad

PROGRESS LOG

Part Coloured	Day and date Achieved
Left arm	
Right arm	
Top	
Left Leg	
Right leg	
Head	
Ball	
Left Sock	

A further type of pictorial scheme is particularly useful for older children. It is also suited where you might be proposing complex incentive items, such as trips out, or where several items are offered, one after the other, as rewards. Schemes based on a thermometer figure, commonly used in fundraising efforts, are a good example and I describe a scheme developed for Tom by his parents.

> *Tom and his parents devised a scheme to work on a sleep problem of his which was getting worse. At eleven years of age, Tom had started to wake during the night and go to his parents' bedroom. At first, he would go back to his own bed with some persuasion, but more recently, he had refused to return and spent most nights in the parental bed. Tom had been an anxious boy at bedtime for several years. A nightlight had helped, as had leaving the bedroom door open. He also valued a settling down time in bed with Mum or Dad before going off to sleep which usually involved reading a story to him. He said he feared intruders and monsters and that these fears were getting worse. There were no other obvious reasons for his insecurities nor did he show any other significant fears. He had however, recently started at a new school, but seemed to be getting on well there. Jill and David, Tom's parents, devised a reward based scheme using a range of items as incentives, as a way of changing the **consequences** for Tom. They drew this out on a sheet of paper and posted it on the kitchen wall. The scheme involved Tom getting three points if, on any night, he did not go into his parents' room.*

If he felt he had to, he would still get one point by returning to his room after a cuddle, and staying there. Tom was enthusiastic about the scheme from the outset, especially because he had thought of most of the reward items. That was not before he had advocated a number of very expensive items, which parents, with good humour, had rejected. The scheme worked well in the first week and Tom stayed in his room on four out of seven nights. On one particular night, he went into parents but returned to his room after five minutes. He got sixteen points in the first week out of a possible maximum of twenty-one points. The second week was less good with twelve points earned, but the target behaviour was still better than before the scheme was started. After six weeks, Tom had settled into a reasonably acceptable pattern of sleeping. It became rare for him to enter his parents' bedroom. He tended to wake as before, but would stay in his bedroom and try to go off to sleep by himself.

Successful Parenting - The Four Step Approach

TOM'S REWARD SCHEME

REWARD POINTS	
100	PAIR OF TRAINERS
95	
90	SPEEDO FOR MY BIKE
85	
80	GRANDAD TO TAKE ME FISHING
75	
70	£10 TO SPEND
65	
60	A LEICESTER CITY FOOTBALL
55	
50	NEW GAME FOR GAMEBOY
45	
40	A NEW LEIC CITY TOP
35	
30	GO SWIMMING WITH JAMES
25	
20	RENT A VIDEO
15	
10	HAVE A SPECIAL STORY READ BY DAD
5	

Allowances

AllowancesThis seems to be a good point to talk about allowances or 'pocket money' for young people. I will avoid the wrath of parents or young people by avoiding the issue of making recommendations for appropriate rates. You will have to make this judgement based on market forces and the results of your negotiating skills. In general, I favour providing young people with allowances at the earliest opportunity. Allowances are an important way of encouraging young people to develop appropriate habits and standards of behaviour, added to which, it helps develop skills in managing money including budgeting, saving and obtaining value for money. They will of, course, make mistakes – sometimes bad ones, but it is far better they squander modest sums at an early age than huge sums as adults.

I favour dividing the allowance into two parts. There should be a set amount, which your child gets in a guaranteed way. It is one that you should agree never to withdraw and considered a 'right'. The other portion can be earned through such activities as doing chores and generally helping to contribute to the smooth operation of the household and family life. This could be withdrawn at any time if the young person fails to meet their agreed obligations. Clearly, the level of the allowance needs to be at a level appropriate to your child's age, and as they get older, the nature of the contribution and the allowance will rise accordingly. You must make it clear that the earned element is dependant on them doing the agreed chores or whatever has been negotiated. If they don't keep their side of the deal-tough, no payment should be given.

Punishment

Punishment techniques can be helpful in supporting parenting objectives but should to be used very sparingly and sensibly. The main reason to be cautious is that they can generate resentment in young people (and in all of us for that matter) which in turn, lessens the effectiveness of punishments and even any reward based approaches which you may be running at the same time. What typically happens is that parents use punishment, find it works, but unfortunately thereafter, find that it *increases* the rate of non-compliant behaviour. They try punishment again, but find it is becoming less effective, and so use more severe or frequent punishment. This works for a time, but again, the probability of even higher rates of non-compliant behaviour occurs. You can see that this is a vicious, downward spiralling trend going nowhere. The trouble is that many parents fail to see this and remain puzzled by the ineffectiveness. They then wonder if there is something 'wrong' with their child and that is when I see them in my clinics.

Defined in psychological terms, a *punisher* is an event that acts in the opposite way to a *reinforcer*. It *reduces* the probability of a particular response occurring. An important thing to keep in mind with all punishments (and rewards for that matter), is that you should try to implement them as quickly as possible after the target behaviour has occurred. Sometimes this is impractical, but even then, you can verbally inform your child at the time, that the punishment will happen at such and such a time. Your words then serve as a type of punishment because they will be backed up with the real thing later.

For practical purposes, I would encourage you to use two main types of punishment. The first is based on withdrawing privileges, a type of negative reinforcement and the second, the application of something that is moderately aversive, sufficient to reduce the undesirable behaviour. With both types remember to record the frequency of the target behaviours both before and after you implement your strategy.

1. Withdrawing Privileges

This strategy involves withdrawing something that is potentially or usually rewarding. Thus for many children, watching a favourite TV programme is pleasurable to the extent that if you deprived them of it, they would find it aversive. This then, is another technique, but I tend to suggest using this sparingly because, as with all punishment techniques, it can create resentment.

Let me illustrate this with common examples for different age groups.

With children (under 11 years of age), using withdrawal of privileges is useful when you are having difficulty in getting your child to behave appropriately in certain very difficult situations. This is usually, when they are being aggressive, very challenging or very disruptive **and** when reward based approaches are either impractical or ineffective. Using it in such a restrained way is more rational to a young person and causes less resentment because they can usually see the logic. Thus if he or she is disrupting other family members when watching television, you could withdraw their right to watch it at that moment. The implementation of the punishment can be delayed if needed. Thus if your child is behaving badly when friends or neighbours visit, for example, you can threaten to withdraw TV privileges later. In such cases, always give the child two or three verbal warnings that you are about to do this to give them a chance at developing self-control. Also, as with many punishment related techniques, keep a sense of proportion. Inappropriate behaviour, such as being rude or attention seeking, should invoke the loss of one favourite programme but not a complete ban on TV for one week. The other reason for keeping sanctions in proportion is to leave you with scope to impose more if you have to. If you ban TV for a week, what do you resort to next?

Another common scenario involving older teenagers is their staying out later than agreed in the evenings. A reasonable way of responding to this is to deny them the privilege of going out on a subsequent occasion or cutting short the time that they are allowed out. Again, it would not be sensible to ban the young person for going out for a whole month unless there was a very serious incident or there had been many previous warnings and violations of the agreed rules.

For a younger teenager, problems such as the refusal to do school homework seem to be a common problem. If your ABC analysis suggests that you need to do something about the consequences, then withdrawal-punishment techniques may be of use. Again, withdrawing a favourite activity is likely to be effective and seen as appropriate by your child. After all, you are criticising the use of their time and their failure to set priorities and so withdrawing a favoured activity is proportionate and reasonable. If on the other hand, for example, you deducted money from an allowance that they were expecting as a right; this would, most likely, be seen as unreasonable. Why should not doing homework result in a loss of money? Part of the power of withdrawal punishment is that, used appropriately, the logic and appropriateness can readily be accepted by young people. They still may not comply, but then you need to re-assess, using the **ABC** approach, and try again.

2. Punishing Events

I need to stress that punishment does not necessarily mean using force or physical violence. Psychologists use the term to describe an action which has the effect of reducing the probability of a given behaviour occurring. Many type of action are punishing without being physically, emotionally, or psychologically harmful.

I generally advise using the application of non-violent and non-harmful types of punishment for stopping a particular type of behaviour occurring when there isn't time or it's not appropriate to delay taking action. A typical scenario is aggressive behaviour towards younger siblings. In a situation such as this, you often do not have the luxury of implementing a reinforcement programme and, you also have to take steps to protect your other child. It is quite possible that in the early stages of trying to reduce this aggressive behaviour, you will have tried reward-based techniques as well as changing antecedent and background events, but without success. After you have done your ABC and feel that a punishment might be of help, try using the mildest one possible, which you feel, is likely to bring about change. A two year old who is aggressive to a brother or sister might, for example, respond to a verbal reprimand.

Verbal Reprimands

Verbal reprimands are a useful form of punishment and can be very effective if you follow some simple rules. As with the other techniques, be clear about what behaviour you are trying to change and keep in mind the following:-

- Don't shout across the room to deliver the reprimand, but get close up to your child so that your face occupies at least 50% of their field of vision.
- Use a level of voice and a tone that your child will find unpleasant and is sufficient to keep their attention. Don't go over the top to hysterical levels, since this will tend to detract from the issue you are trying to address - your child will spend more time trying to make sense of your overreaction instead of reflecting on the inappropriateness of their behaviour.
- Keep your remarks to the point such as, "No, you mustn't do that". Afterwards, do not make the mistake of giving him or her a big hug or smiling, as this just becomes confusing. Try to keep a neutral, matter of fact expression and return to normal after 15 minutes or more, as feels appropriate.

Time Out

This is particularly useful for children in early to late childhood. The phrase 'Time Out' is short for 'Time-out from reinforcement'. In other words, the punishment element is removing the child from a place they would normally find rewarding. In practice, at least for younger children, it is usually a family room in the home particularly one containing other family members, or caregivers, or where activities such as watching TV takes place. The technique is most usefully employed when there is an issue about the child's conduct in the home and he or she is present in the room where there are pleasurable or reinforcing events occurring. He or she may be being disruptive, destructive, and aggressive or refusing to comply with a reasonable request.

One of the good things about Time Out is that in addition to being a useful punishment, it teaches self-control. It does this in two ways. First, you give your child a chance to moderate their behaviour before you implement Time Out. Second, when they are in Time Out, it must be for a set time, which may be extended if they are still showing undesirable behaviour i.e. having a temper tantrum or being destructive. In other words, to come out of Time Out, they must have ceased displaying the undesirable behaviour.

It comes as a surprise to many parents to learn that some undesirable behaviour from a child can be reinforced i.e. encouraged, by their angry reactions. For some children in some situations, just getting Mum wound up can be satisfying.

This is a very common presentation in mothers who are suffering from a Depressive Disorder and with children who have Attention Deficit Hyperactive Disorder (ADHD). Depressed Mums have to battle with needing to withdraw socially and yet at home, meeting the needs of children. This sometimes doesn't work out and children can learn to force mothers to engage with them through outrageous behaviour. Children with ADHD have an above average need for stimulus. If it is a little boring at home, they can easily liven things up with any behaviour that provokes a reaction. These are special cases, but illustrate how parents can unwittingly reinforce inappropriate behaviour. Keep in mind however, that this tendency applies to all children. There are of course other reasons behind challenging behaviour that you will try to identify using the **ABC** approach. For example, a key background factor for many young people is just plain anger. As commonly is the case, if they can't resolve some problem they have, their anger is vented on parents. Your **ABC** analysis should be helpful in trying to identify if there is such a key background factor at work. You will then need to work on this, but in the meantime, it may be important to bring inappropriate behaviour quickly under control using Time Out, especially if the behaviour is badly affecting family life or threatening your own mental health.

There are again, a few simple rules to follow.

1. Time Out should be brief. I suggest no more than 1 minute for every year of your child's age i.e. 8 minutes for an 8 year old.

2. Time Out should be implemented away from what is assumed to be a reinforcing situation such as a room where the undesirable behaviour is occurring. The Time-Out place can be the hall, stairs, or another room. The important thing to remember is that the environment must be safe. It shouldn't be an overly boring environment nor should it be overly pleasurable. Quite often, your child's bedroom is a good place to use. It is usually safe, it is an acceptable environment for your child, and there may be some things for them to do to occupy themselves. At first sight, this may seem the wrong thing to do but remember; the punishment element is to remove them from the place where they are getting some reinforcement. You do not need a double punishment by putting them in an unfriendly, unstimulating or hostile environment.

3. Before you ever resort to Time Out, give your child two or three warnings that you will be invoking Time Out unless they comply. This is really important because at the end of the day, you are trying to teach your child self-control so give them a chance to develop it.

4. Implement Time-Out in a calm matter of fact way. Don't get angry but looking annoyed is fine. After Time-Out has ended, stay neutral for a while and resist the temptation for excessive signs of approval such as hugs, praise etc.

5. The most difficult part of Time Out is what to do if your child opposes going to, or staying in, Time Out. Children will naturally learn a number of strategies to avoid it: promising, "not to do it", wanting to go to the toilet, or continuing a temper tantrum etc. It is very tempting to give into this but remember, that would be allowing your child to overturn the terms you have laid down. That will not teach self-control or compliance but instead, will teach the child the value of challenging and opposing you.

6. Make it clear that in going into Time-Out, you expect your child to cease any temper tantrum or engage in any other disruptive or destructive behaviour. If such behaviour is present at the scheduled end time, then they must repeat the Time Out. The same applies again, if in the second Time Out, the third Time Out and beyond the rules continue to be broken.

7. Be warned that in applying time out, the target behaviour might get worse before it gets better. The reason for this is fairly easy to see. Up to the point that you might implement Time Out, your child has been the one in control. No one gives up control that easily. In addition, your child may have learned that if they are stubborn, persistent and determined enough, they will get their own way. Hence, when you start to introduce the sanction, there is likely to be a battle of wills. You might find that you have to repeat Time Out several times in succession because your child refuses to stay

in Time Out for the set time. Don't despair at this point but persist and you will notice that the frequency of the undesirable behaviour drops and with it the need for Time Out.

8. As with most of these strategies I am outlining, they work best if they are devised in advance of likely problems occurring as opposed to trying to work them out on the spot.

9. As with all of the strategies, keep a record of before and after so that you know if you are effective. Remember to share this with your child.

Physical punishment

Increasingly, this method of discipline is seen as socially unacceptable. Currently the law in the UK allows for "reasonable chastisement" by parents but even this is, according to a Joint Parliamentary Committee of British Members of Parliament, is at variance with the UN convention on the rights of the child, and breaches a ruling by the European Court of Human Rights (Guardian, 2003). Things came to a head in 1998 when the European Court of Human Rights ruled that the British law on corporal punishment in the home failed to protect children's rights, after considering the case of a boy who had been beaten by his stepfather with a three-foot garden cane between the ages of five and eight years. The stepfather was acquitted by a British court of causing actual bodily harm. He had argued that the beating was "reasonable chastisement". The most recent development in the UK is some further clarification in Section 58 of the Children Act 2004, which came into force on 15 January 2005. This however, still allows the use of "reasonable punishment" and so, the law as it stands, still quite rightly in my view, attracts the wrath of many lobbing groups.

Aside from this move to outlaw smacking, I believe there are objections on psychological grounds.

1. There are many other strategies parents can use, to encourage children to comply with reasonable parental requests and expectations. I have dealt with the most useful in this book and generally, positive parenting techniques using praise and encouragement work extremely well.

2. Physical punishments have the disadvantage of causing resentment in children and can badly affect their emotional attachments to parents. I am not convinced by the arguments that you can stress to the child that it is not they you are punishing, but their behaviour - that although you are going to hit them, you still love them. This type of argument is for example, outlined by Dr James Dobson (1978) in his book "Parenting the Strong Willed Child".

3. Good parenting is about teaching children effective and acceptable ways of solving social problems. This is why we generally do not, for example, condone bullying in schools and the workplace. It becomes confusing to

a child if you use physical chastisement at home as a way of solving your parenting problems.

4. Physical punishment tends not to work because it causes resentment, which then increases the probability of your child opposing you again. You are then in danger of having to escalate the severity of punishment which then causes more resentment and undesirable behaviour which becomes even more challenging. This is what causes many parents to become locked into a habit of physical punishment which can go on for years. Approximately eighty children every year in the UK die from physical abuse from family members. Strangers kill three or four. Using physical punishment can run in families from one generation to the next and usually gets worse at it progresses. If you can, stop it with your generation – Don't pass it on.

Even with the best will in the world parents' occasionally, to use their own words, "smack", "tap", "hit" or give their children a "clip round the ear". This more often than not arises from frustration. Commonly, they tell me that they were "at the end of my tether" In many instances, physical punishment is not the first resort of parents, but the last or done in times of desperation. The main way to avoid this situation is to use the reinforcement strategies outlined here as well as using other types of non-physical punishment techniques sparingly.

WHEN TO SEEK PROFESSIONAL HELP

I hope by now that above all, you feel that although parenting is tough and challenging, like most other skills, it can be developed with a little bit of effort, steel like nerves and infinite patience. That said, you might need outside help from time to time. Most commonly, this will be provided by family, friends, and others who have care of your children such as school staff. If you find that more help is needed, it may be the time to think about seeking professional help. This is quite a big barrier for many parents to overcome but if you have tried to solve the issues and have failed after determined attempts, then do consider seeking help. There may be specific techniques, which can be of help, but your child may be suffering from a mental health disorder, which, if left untreated, may compromise their general development and psychosocial adjustment.

The extent of the help available varies enormously. In the UK, there are a growing number of mental health professionals available. Your general practitioner is the key source of information and help but remember Health Visitors, School Nurses and Voluntary agencies are also there to help. Please visit the **FOUR-STEP APPROACH** Website at www.FOURSTEPAPPROACH.com for further useful information and contacts.

REFERENCES

Adler (2000) Pigeonholed: New Scientist 167 (2258) 389-341

Caspi A, et al (2003) Children's behavioural styles at age 3 are linked to their adult personality traits at age 26. Journal of Personality. 71(4) 495-513.

Dobson J (1978) The Strong Willed Child. Tyndale House: Illinois.

Eaves, L J et al. (1997) Genetics and Developmental Psychopathology: 2. The Main Effects of Genes and Environment on Behavioural Problems in the Virginia Twins Study of Adolescent behavioural Development.
Journal of Child Psychology and Psychiatry. 38.8. pp 965-980

Friel JC & Friel LD (1999) The Seven Worst Things Parents Do. Deerfield Beach Florida: Health Communications.

Frombonne, E (2003) Epidemiological Surveys of Autism and other Pervasive Developmental Disorders. Journal of Autism & Developmental Disorders. 33(4) 365-382.

Guardian (2003) Leader Article, Wednesday, June 25th

Jaffee, S.R. et al. (2004). The limits of child effects: evidence for genetically mediated child effects on corporal punishment but not on physical maltreatments. Developmental Psychology 40(6) 1047-1058

Raine, A (2002) Annotation: The role of prefrontal deficits, low autonomic arousal, and early health factors in the development of anti-social and aggressive behaviour in children.
Journal of Child Psychology and Psychiatry. 43:4. pp.417-434

Milgram S. (1963) Behavioural study of Obedience. Journal of Abnormal & Social Psychology, 67, 391-398.

Schaffer HR and Emerson PE (1964) The development of social attachments in infancy. Monographs of the Society for Research in Child Development 29.

Sharry, J (2001) Parent Power: bringing up responsible children and teenagers. Chichester:John Wiley

Social Trends (1995) Social Trends 25 years. Central Statistical Office of the UK. London: The Stationery Office.

Social Trends (2002) London: The Stationery Office.

Sunday Telegraph (2003) Article. Schools Chief: Parents have raised worst generation yet. 31st August 2003

Thomas A, Chess S, and Birch HG (1968). Temperament and Behavioural Disorders in Children. New York: University Press.

Turecki S (1989) The Difficult Child New York: Bantam.

Index

A

Aggressiveness 3, 6, 10, 12, 76
Allowances 137
Anxiety xviii, 11, 16, 19, 23, 31, 68, 70
Applied behavioural analysis 95
Asperger's syndrome 74
Attachment 23, 30, 31, 57, 58
Attention Deficit Hyperactivity Disorder 16
Authoritarian parenting 36, 42, 46
Authoritative parenting 41, 42, 47, 49
Authority 8, 9, 37, 38, 41, 48, 85, 86, 90
Autism 2, 74, 151

B

Behaviour xiii, xiv, xv, xvii, xix, xxiii, xxvi, 1, 2, 3, 4, 8, 10, 16, 17, 22, 24, 25, 29, 30, 32, 40, 41, 42, 49, 55, 60, 64, 90, 91, 95, 96, 97, 98, 99, 100, 101, 102, 104, 105, 106, 107, 109, 111, 112, 113, 114, 115, 116, 117, 118, 120, 122, 123, 125, 127, 131, 135, 137, 138, 139, 140, 141, 142, 143, 144, 145, 146, 147, 148, 149, 152
  descriptions of 99
  internalization of standards 41, 42, 137
  limits and standards 40
  non-compliant 60, 90, 138
  recording and measuring 116
Behavioural genetics 2
Behavioural problems xxii, xxvi, 2, 4, 89, 120, 151
  early development of 4
  genetics 16
Bio-psycho-social influences 51
Biological influences 3, 87, 103. *See* Genetics
Birth order 93, 94
Bonding 2, 23, 30. *See* Attachment
Bullying 6, 71, 91, 92, 148

C

Cognitive constructs 25
Culture 2, 63, 82, 83, 84, 86
  child and youth 82, 84

D

Depression xxi, 17
Developmental 19, 20, 59, 75, 83, 88, 89, 94, 97, 103
  disorders 16, 74, 88, 89, 92, 151, 153
  needs 19, 20, 83
Diversity xv, xviii, xix, 12
  and individual differences xix, 11
Dyslexia 19, 72, 73
Dyspraxia 73

E

Early adolescence xxiii, 92
Early childhood xxiii, 3, 131
Emotional 7, 12, 15, 22, 23, 24, 26, 29, 33, 34, 36, 37, 38, 42, 48, 58, 61, 62, 63, 64, 71, 75, 77, 91, 97, 102, 112, 120, 121, 148
  and behavioural disturbance 58
  emotional warmth 36, 37
  stability 12

well-being 48
Encouragement xvi, xx, 54, 67, 71, 115, 119, 120, 121, 122, 123, 124, 148
  and authoritative parenting 41
Epilepsy 88, 90
Evil xx, 8, 10
Evolution 6, 32. *See also* Nature
Expressed warmth 33

F

Family xvii, xix, 5, 18, 33, 34, 36, 40, 45, 46, 49, 51, 52, 53, 55, 56, 63, 64, 77, 78, 79, 82, 85, 91, 94, 103, 108, 111, 121, 127, 128, 137, 140, 143, 144, 149, 150
  changes in xiv, xxvi, 7, 49, 55, 61, 99
  dysfunctional 33
  new relationships 55, 59
  two-parent family 52
Fostering 17, 30, 52

G

Genetics 3, 22
  anxiety 16
  Attention Deficit Hyperactivity Disorder 16
  behavioural problems 16
  height 14
  low resting heart rate 10
  personality types 12
  twin studies 16, 151

H

Heart rate
  low resting and criminality 10
Height 10, 14, 15, 92. *See* Physical characteristics
Higher education xii, 66
  numbers attending xii
  numbers in 66

I

Independence xiii, 20, 24, 34, 35
Individual differences
  respecting 11
Infancy xxiii, 4, 152
  definition of xxiii
Intelligence 7, 12, 18, 65, 72, 80. *See* IQ
  genetics and 7
Introversion 12
Irritability 4, 12, 103, 113
  early problems 4

K

Key moments 43, 44

L

Late childhood xxiii, 34, 59, 143
  definition of xxiii
Learning difficulty 72
Learning disability xiii, 72
Life expectancy xii
Low self-esteem xx, 19, 90, 120, 123, 124

M

Magical thinking 59
Marriage. *See* parental separation and divorce
  abusive experiences 52
  break-up 54
  breakdown 52
  disagreements 47
  duration xii
  marital issues 47
  pressures on xii
  quality 63
  separation 53
  violence and abuse 54
Maternal deprivation 30
Middle childhood xxiii, 125
Morality

development 76
stealing 43, 44, 80, 86
Mothers x, 2, 30, 31, 52, 55, 58, 65, 144
and work x
Motor skills difficulties 73, 74

N

Nature
  human characteristics 14
  individual differences 11
  and nurture 4
Negative comments 33
Neighbourhoods xvii, xxv, 77, 80, 82
Neuroticism 12
Non-resident parent 54, 55, 57, 58, 61
Nursery school xxi, 30, 69

O

Older adolescence
  definition of xxiii
Opposition and rebelliousness 38
Orphanages 30

P

Parental
  overprotection 34, 92
  expectations 17
  values 86
Parental separation and divorce 45
  childrens' intelligence 65
  Childrens' wishes 57
  controlling information to children 62
  critical comments 57
  emotional detachment of children 48
  levels of contact 57
  new partner 61
  and attachment 53

contact visits 59
reduced contact 53, 55
separation 53
Parenting. *See* Authoritative parenting
  appropriate expectations xiii
  blame and guilt culture 2
  effective 15
  ineffectiveness 47
  key moments 43
  overcontroling 46
  overly accommodating 38
  perfect 42
  poor models 40
  rationality 43
  style 23, 35
  style conflicts of 45
  vocabulary 32
  style 59
Parents
  ambitions for children 19
  and own childhood experiences 17
  and taking account of developmental needs 20
  and taking account of skills and personality of children 19
  attachment 29
  blaming of xvi
  expressed warmth 33
  living life through children 21
Permissive parenting 38, 42, 46
  Cold and permissive 40
  Warm and permissive 39
Personality
  differences in 3
  prediction 4
  types 12
Physical characteristics 22, 91
Physical Health Problems 87
Pictorial schemes 131
Point systems 126
Positive parenting xvi, xx, 120, 148

Praise and encouragement 121
 giving by parents 33
Privation 30
Problems
 prioritising 114
Punishment 138
 effects on learning 8
 physical 147
 time-out 143
 types 149
 withdrawing privileges 139

R

Reinforcement 115, 118, 119, 121, 122, 123, 124, 139, 141, 143, 145, 149. *See* Token Systems; *See* Star charts; *See* Pictorial schemes; *See* Point Systems
Relationships
 formal xxv, 78, 79, 80, 86
 informal 79
 undesirable 82
Religion 85
 religious groups 78
Resident parent 54, 55, 57, 58, 61
Resilience 14, 30
Rewards
 short-term 39
 strategy 45

S

Schizophrenia 2, 28
School 66
 bullying 71
 difficulties with 68
 expectations at 39
 numbers in higher education x
 positives 66
 proportion of children attending x
 UK Chief Inspector of x
Self-control 39, 140, 143, 145, 146
Self-discipline 42
Self-esteem xiv, xx, 19, 42, 81, 88, 89, 90, 91, 120, 123, 124
Shouting 36, 98, 111
Sibling relationships 93, 94
Single parents xii, 52
 households 40
Skills
 strenghening 15
Sleep
 early problems 4
Social
 changes xii
 competence 77
 rejection 91
 relationships 29, 97
 evaluation 29
Star charts ix, 125
Stature 91, 92
Stealing 43, 44, 80, 86
Stereotypes 27, 28, 29
Stress 48, 59, 60, 63, 65, 74, 103, 104, 113, 141, 148
Substance abuse
 Solvents 80

T

Talk
 positive and negative 32
Teachers. *See* Schools
Temperament 4, 15, 19, 67, 75
Temper tantrums 17, 18, 114
Templates 24, 26, 27, 29
Time Out ix, 111, 143, 144, 145, 146, 147
Token systems 121, 124, 125, 131
Torture 8
TV xi, 28, 82, 84, 108, 109, 111, 124, 139, 140, 143

Twins xviii, 16, 22, 65, 94

U

University xii, 8, 153

V

Violence 5, 9, 45, 46, 48, 53, 54, 64, 65, 141
  impact on IQ 65
Visual perception 24
Voluntary organizations 78

W

War 5, 6, 8, 12
Women
  life expectancy xii
Worry 7, 19, 68, 70, 80, 95

Y

Young people x, xii, xiii, xvi, xx, xxi, xxii, xxiii, xxiv, xxvi, 3, 10, 14, 16, 20, 23, 24, 29, 30, 32, 34, 35, 36, 37, 38, 41, 42, 43, 47, 48, 51, 56, 57, 62, 63, 66, 73, 76, 77, 78, 79, 80, 82, 83, 84, 85, 86, 87, 89, 91, 92, 96, 97, 100, 102, 103, 115, 120, 121, 123, 128, 137, 138, 141, 144

Printed in Great Britain
by Amazon.co.uk, Ltd.,
Marston Gate.